D0687659

GRAPHIS LETTERHEAD 3

GRAPHIS LETTERHEAD 3

· ·

(OPPOSITE) PHOTOGRAPHER: R.J. MUNA

AN INTERNATIONAL COLLECTION OF LETTERHEAD DESIGN

BRIEFPAPIERGESTALTUNG IM INTERNATIONALEN ÜBERBLICK

UNE COMPILATION INTERNATIONALE SUR LE DESIGN DE PAPIERS À LETTRES

EDITED BY · HERAUSGEGEBEN VON · EDITÉ PAR:

B. MARTIN PEDERSEN

PUBLISHER AND CREATIVE DIRECTOR: B. MARTIN PEDERSEN

EDITORS: ANNETTE CRANDALL, HEINKE JENSSEN

ASSOCIATE EDITOR: JÖRG REIMANN

ART DIRECTORS: B. MARTIN PEDERSEN, RANDELL PEARSON

PHOTOGRAPHER: ALFREDO PARRAGA

GRAPHIS U.S., INC. NEW YORK, GRAPHIS PRESS CORP. ZÜRICH (SWITZERLAND)

CONTENTS

INHALT

SOMMAIRE

REMARKS

WE EXTEND OUR HEARTFELT THANKS TO CONTRIBUTORS THROUGHOUT THE WORLD WHO HAVE MADE IT POSSIBLE TO PUBLISH A WIDE AND INTERNATIONAL SPECTRUM OF THE BEST WORK IN THIS FIELD.

ENTRY INSTRUCTIONS FOR ALL GRAPHIS BOOKS MAY BE REQUESTED AT:
GRAPHIS PRESS
141 LEXINGTON AVENUE
NEW YORK, NY 10016-8193

ANMERKUNGEN

UNSER DANK GILT DEN EINSENDERN AUS ALLER WELT, DIE ES UNS DURCH IHRE BEITRÄGE ERMÖGLICHT HABEN, EIN BREITES, INTERNATIONALES SPEKTRUM DER BESTEN ARBEITEN ZU VERÖFFENTLICHEN.

TEILNAHMEBEDINGUNGEN FÜR DIE GRAPHISBÜCHER SIND ERHÄLTLICH BEIM:
GRAPHIS VERLAG AG
DUFOURSTRASSE 107
8008 ZÜRICH, SCHWEIZ

ANNOTATIONS

TOUTE NOTRE RECONNAISSANCE VA AUX DESIGNERS DU MONDE ENTIER DONT LES ENVOIS NOUS ONT PERMIS DE CONSTITUER UN VASTE PANORAMA INTERNATIONAL DES MEILLEURES CRÉATIONS.

LES MODALITÉS D'INSCRIPTION PEUVENT ÊTRE OBTENUES AUPRÉS DE:
EDITIONS GRAPHIS
DUFOURSTRASSE 107
8008 ZÜRICH, SUISSE

(OPPOSITE) PHOTOGRAPHER: DAVID O'CONNOR ■ (PAGE 224) PHOTOGRAPHER: FRANCINE ZASLOW

GRAPHIS PUBLICATIONS

GRAPHIS, THE INTERNATIONAL BI-MONTHLY JOURNAL OF VISUAL COMMUNICATION

GRAPHIS SHOPPING BAG, AN INTERNATIONAL COLLECTION OF SHOPPING BAG DESIGN

GRAPHIS MUSIC CD, AN INTERNATIONAL COLLECTION OF CD DESIGN

GRAPHIS BOOK DESIGN, AN INTERNATIONAL COLLECTION OF BOOK DESIGN

GRAPHIS DESIGN, THE INTERNATIONAL ANNUAL OF DESIGN AND ILLUSTRATION

GRAPHIS ADVERTISING, THE INTERNATIONAL ANNUAL OF ADVERTISING

GRAPHIS BROCHURES, A COMPILATION OF BROCHURE DESIGN

GRAPHIS PHOTO, THE INTERNATIONAL ANNUAL OF PHOTOGRAPHY

GRAPHIS ALTERNATIVE PHOTOGRAPHY, THE INTERNATIONAL ANNUAL OF ALTERNATIVE PHOTOGRAPHY

GRAPHIS NUDES, A COLLECTION OF CAREFULLY SELECTED SOPHISTICATED IMAGES

GRAPHIS POSTER, THE INTERNATIONAL ANNUAL OF POSTER ART

GRAPHIS PACKAGING, AN INTERNATIONAL COMPILATION OF PACKAGING DESIGN

GRAPHIS LETTERHEAD, AN INTERNATIONAL COMPILATION OF LETTERHEAD DESIGN

GRAPHIS DIAGRAM, THE GRAPHIC VISUALIZATION OF ABSTRACT, TECHNICAL AND STATISTICAL FACTS AND FUNCTIONS

GRAPHIS LOGO, AN INTERNATIONAL COMPILATION OF LOGOS

GRAPHIS EPHEMERA, AN INTERNATIONAL COLLECTION OF PROMOTIONAL ART

GRAPHIS PUBLICATION, AN INTERNATIONAL SURVEY OF THE BEST IN MAGAZINE DESIGN

GRAPHIS ANNUAL REPORTS, AN INTERNATIONAL COMPILATION OF THE BEST DESIGNED ANNUAL REPORTS

GRAPHIS CORPORATE IDENTITY, AN INTERNATIONAL COMPILATION OF THE BEST IN CORPORATE IDENTITY DESIGN

GRAPHIS TYPOGRAPHY, AN INTERNATIONAL COMPILATION OF THE BEST IN TYPOGRAPHIC DESIGN

GRAPHIS PUBLIKATIONEN

GRAPHIS, DIE INTERNATIONALE ZWEIMONATSZEITSCHRIFT DER VISUELLEN KOMMUNIKATION

GRAPHIS SHOPPING BAG, TRAGTASCHEN-DESIGN IM INTERNATIONALEN ÜBERBLICK

GRAPHIS MUSIC CD, CD-DESIGN IM INTERNATIONALEN ÜBERBLICK

GRAPHIS BOOKS, BUCHGESTALTUNG IM INTERNATIONALEN ÜBERBLICK

GRAPHIS DESIGN, DAS INTERNATIONALE JAHRBUCH ÜBER DESIGN UND ILLUSTRATION

GRAPHIS ADVERTISING, DAS INTERNATIONALE JAHRBUCH DER WERBUNG

GRAPHIS BROCHURES, BROSCHÜRENDESIGN IM INTERNATIONAL ÜBERBLICK

GRAPHIS PHOTO, DAS INTERNATIONALE JAHRBUCH DER PHOTOGRAPHIE

GRAPHIS ALTERNATIVE PHOTOGRAPHY, DAS INTERNATIONALE JAHRBUCH ÜBER ALTERNATIVE PHOTOGRAPHIE

GRAPHIS NUDES, EINE SAMMLUNG SORGFÄLTIG AUSGEWÄHLTER AKTPHOTOGRAPHIE

GRAPHIS POSTER, DAS INTERNATIONALE JAHRBUCH DER PLAKATKUNST

GRAPHIS PACKAGING, EIN INTERNATIONALER ÜBERBLICK ÜBER DIE PACKUNGSGESTALTUNG

GRAPHIS LETTERHEAD, EIN INTERNATIONALER ÜBERBLICK ÜBER BRIEFPAPIERGESTALTUNG

GRAPHIS DIAGRAM, DIE GRAPHISCHE DARSTELLUNG ABSTRAKTER TECHNISCHER UND STATISTISCHER DATEN UND FAKTEN

GRAPHIS LOGO, EINE INTERNATIONALE AUSWAHL VON FIRMEN-LOGOS

GRAPHIS EPHEMERA, EINE INTERNATIONALE SAMMLUNG GRAPHISCHER DOKUMENTE DES TÄGLICHEN LEBENS

GRAPHIS MAGAZINDESIGN, EINE INTERNATIONALE ZUSAMMENSTELLUNG DES BESTEN ZEITSCHRIFTEN-DESIGNS

GRAPHIS ANNUAL REPORTS, EIN INTERNATIONALER ÜBERBLICK ÜBER DIE GESTALTUNG VON JAHRESBERICHTEN

GRAPHIS CORPORATE IDENTITY, EINE INTERNATIONALE AUSWAHL DES BESTEN CORPORATE IDENTITY DESIGNS

GRAPHIS TYPOGRAPHY, EINE INTERNATIONALE ZUSAMMENSTELLUNG DES BESTEN TYPOGRAPHIE DESIGN

PUBLICATIONS GRAPHIS

GRAPHIS, LA REVUE BIMESTRIELLE INTERNATIONALE DE LA COMMUNICATION VISUELLE

GRAPHIS SHOPPING BAG, UNE COMPILATION INTERNATIONALE SUR LE DESIGN DES SACS À COMMISSIONS

GRAPHIS MUSIC CD, UNE COMPILATION INTERNATIONALE SUR LE DESIGN DES CD

GRAPHIS BOOKS, UNE COMPILATION INTERNATIONALE SUR LE DESIGN DES LIVRES

GRAPHIS DESIGN, LE RÉPERTOIRE INTERNATIONAL DE LA COMMUNICATION VISUELLE

GRAPHIS ADVERTISING, LE RÉPERTOIRE INTERNATIONAL DE LA PUBLICITÉ

GRAPHIS BROCHURES, UNE COMPILATION INTERNATIONALE SUR LE DESIGN DES BROCHURES

GRAPHIS PHOTO, LE RÉPERTOIRE INTERNATIONAL DE LA PHOTOGRAPHIE

GRAPHIS ALTERNATIVE PHOTOGRAPHY, LE RÉPERTOIRE INTERNATIONAL DE LA PHOTOGRAPHIE ALTERNATIVE

GRAPHIS NUDES, UN FLORILÈGE DE LA PHOTOGRAPHIE DE NUS

GRAPHIS POSTER, LE RÉPERTOIRE INTERNATIONAL DE L'AFFICHE

GRAPHIS PACKAGING, LE RÉPERTOIRE INTERNATIONAL DE LA CRÉATION D'EMBALLAGES

GRAPHIS LETTERHEAD, LE RÉPERTOIRE INTERNATIONAL DU DESIGN DE PAPIER À LETTRES

GRAPHIS DIAGRAM, LE RÉPERTOIRE GRAPHIQUE DE FAITS ET DONNÉES ABSTRAITS, TECHNIQUES ET STATISTIQUES

GRAPHIS LOGO, LE RÉPERTOIRE INTERNATIONAL DU LOGO

GRAPHIS EPHEMERA, LE GRAPHISME – UN ÉTAT D'ESPRIT AU QUOTIDIEN

GRAPHIS PUBLICATION, LE RÉPERTOIRE INTERNATIONAL DU DESIGN DE PÉRIODIQUES

GRAPHIS ANNUAL REPORTS, PANORAMA INTERNATIONAL DU MEILLEUR DESIGN DE RAPPORTS ANNUELS D'ENTREPRISES

GRAPHIS CORPORATE IDENTITY, PANORAMA INTERNATIONAL DU MEILLEUR DESIGN D'IDENTITÉ CORPORATE

GRAPHIS TYPOGRAPHY, LE RÉPERTOIRE INTERNATIONAL DU MEILLEUR DESIGN DE TYPOGRAPHIE

PUBLICATION NO. 260 (ISBN 1-888001-03-8)

© COPYRIGHT UNDER UNIVERSAL COPYRIGHT CONVENTION

COPYRIGHT © 1996 BY GRAPHIS U.S., NEW YORK, GRAPHIS PRESS CORP., ZURICH, SWITZERLAND

JACKET AND BOOK DESIGN COPYRIGHT © 1996 BY PEDERSEN DESIGN

141 LEXINGTON AVENUE, NEW YORK, N.Y. 10016 USA

NO PART OF THIS BOOK MAY BE REPRODUCED IN ANY FORM WITHOUT WRITTEN
PERMISSION OF THE PUBLISHER

PRINTED IN HONG KONG BY PARAMOUNT PRINTING COMPANY LIMITED

Strathmore

GRAPHIS LETTERHEAD 3

HAS BEEN PRODUCED IN CONJUNCTION WITH
THE "STRATHMORE PRESENTS GRAPHIS" LETTERHEAD EXHIBITION
AND THROUGH THE GENEROUS SUPPORT OF
STRATHMORE PAPERS.

GRAPHIS LETTERHEAD 3

WURDE MIT FREUNDLICHER UNTERSTÜTZUNG VON
STRATHMORE PAPERS UND IN VERBINDUNG MIT DER AUSSTELLUNG
«STRATHMORE PRESENTS GRAPHIS»
PRODUZIERT.

GRAPHIS LETTERHEAD 3

A ÉTÉ PRODUIT EN COOPERATION AVEC
L'EXPOSITION INTITULÉE «STRATHMORE PRESENTS GRAPHIS»
ET GRACE AU SOUTIEN GÉNÉREUX DE
STRATHMORE PAPERS.

Stationery in the Age of E-mail?

Read the papers. Watch the news. Something big is afoot. Technological advances are radically changing how we live and how we work — advances based most profoundly on how we communicate. ❂ "Call me on my cell' phone, or E-mail it and I'll get it later. Fax me. Maybe you can modem it. Later, we'll have a virtual meeting . . ." ❂ In this environment, some people may lose sight of the things that have been around for a while, things like ink and paper. We think it's important that they don't. ❂ Because amidst today's array of electronic "realities", the things you can actually reach out and touch seem that much more special — and important. Real things, like a crisp sheet of paper in your hands. ❂ That's why those important documents are still on stationery, actual stationery. And why they'll continue to be. ❂ Strathmore is sponsoring the book and travelling exhibition of *Graphis Letterhead 3* because we believe there is, and will continue to be, an important place for good design, good printing and good paper in this increasingly wired world.

SCHAUEN SIE IN DIE ZEITUNGEN. SEHEN SIE DIE TV-NACHRICHTEN. ES IST ETWAS GROSSES IM GANGE. TECHNOLOGISCHE ENTWICKLUNGEN VERÄNDERN RADIKAL UNSERE ARBEITS- UND LEBENSWEISE — UND ZWAR VOR ALLEM UNSERE ART ZU KOMMUNIZIEREN. ❂ «RUFEN SIE MICH AUF MEINEM MOBILTELEPHON AN, ODER SCHICKEN SIE MIR ES PER E-MAIL ODER PER FAX. VIELLEICHT KÖNNEN SIE ES PER MODEM SCHICKEN. SPÄTER WERDEN WIR EINE VIRTUELLE KONFERENZ HABEN...» ❂ IN DIESEM UMFELD WERDEN MANCHE LEUTE VIELLEICHT EINIGE DINGE VERGESSEN, DIE ES SCHON LANGE GIBT: DINGE WIE TINTE UND PAPIER. WIR FINDEN ES WICHTIG, DASS SIE SIE NICHT VERGESSEN. ❂

DENN MITTEN IN DEN ELEKTRONISCHEN «REALITÄTEN» UNSERER ZEIT ERSCHEINEN DIE DINGE, DIE WIR TATSÄCHLICH IN DIE HAND NEHMEN UND SPÜREN KÖNNEN ALS ETWAS BESONDERES — UND WICHTIGES. RICHTIGE DINGE WIE EIN BLATT PAPIER IN UNSEREN HÄNDEN. ❂ AUS DIESEM GRUNDE SIND WICHTIGE DOKUMENTE NOCH IMMER AUF PAPIER, RICHTIGEM PAPIER. UND DAS WIRD AUCH WEITERHIN SO SEIN. ❂ STRATHMORE SPONSERT DIESES BUCH UND DIE WANDERAUSSTELLUNG VON *GRAPHIS LETTERHEAD 3*, WEIL WIR GLAUBEN, DASS ES IN DIESER ZUNEHMEND VERKABELTEN WELT NOCH IMMER EINEN WICHTIGEN PLATZ FÜR GUTE GESTALTUNG, GUTE DRUCKQUALITÄT UND GUTES PAPIER GIBT UND GEBEN WIRD.

SI VOUS LISEZ LES JOURNAUX ET SI VOUS REGARDEZ LES INFORMATIONS, VOUS CONSTATEREZ QU'UNE RÉVOLUTION EST EN MARCHE. LES NOUVELLES TECHNOLOGIES SONT EN TRAIN DE MODIFIER NOTRE MANIÈRE DE VIVRE ET DE TRAVAILLER ET ELLES TRANSFORMENT NOTRE FAÇON DE COMMUNIQUER. ❂ «APPELLE-MOI SUR LE TÉLÉPHONE CELLULAIRE — LAISSE UN MESSAGE SUR L'E-MAIL — ENVOIE-MOI UN FAX. PEUT-ÊTRE QUE TU POURRAIS LE TRANSFÉRER PAR MODEM? UN PEU PLUS TARD NOUS AURONS UNE CONFÉRENCE VIRTUELLE...». ❂ DANS CE TYPE D'ENVIRONNEMENT, CERTAINES PERSONNES POURRAIENT OUBLIER L'EXISTENCE D'OBJETS QUI

POURRAIENT ONT SERVI L'HUMANITÉ DEPUIS DES MILLÉNAIRES, COMME PAR EXEMPLE L'ENCRE ET LE PAPIER. ❂ NOUS SOMMES D'AVIS QU'À L'ÈRE DU TOUT-ÉLECTRONIQUE ET DE LA RÉALITÉ VIRTUELLE, LES OBJETS QUE L'ON PEUT TOUCHER — COMME LA FEUILLE DE PAPIER QUI CRISSE SOUS LES DOIGTS — PRENNENT D'AUTANT PLUS DE VALEUR. ❂ STRATHMORE PAPER COMPANY SPONSORISE LE LIVRE AINSI QUE L'EXPOSITION ITINÉRANTE *GRAPHIS LETTERHEAD 3*, PARCE QUE NOUS SOMMES CONVAINCUS QU'IL Y A ET QU'IL CONTINUERA À Y AVOIR UNE PLACE DE CHOIX POUR LE BON DESIGN, L'IMPRESSION ET LE PAPIER DE QUALITÉ DANS UN UNIVERS DE PLUS EN PLUS IMMATÉRIEL.

STRATHMORE IS A REGISTERED TRADEMARK OF INTERNATIONAL PAPER COMPANY

Strathmore Papers

AWARD WINNERS

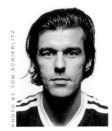

BEST LETTERHEAD ON STRATHMORE PAPER
ART DIRECTOR: STEFAN SAGMEISTER
CLIENT: TOTO NEW CONCEPT GROUP (PAGE 139)

BEST US LETTERHEAD
ART DIRECTOR: JOE DUFFY
CLIENT: DUFFY N.Y.C. (PAGE 61)

BEST EUROPEAN LETTERHEAD
ART DIRECTORS: PAUL POSTMA (LEFT) AND JACQUES KOEWEIDEN (RIGHT)
CLIENT: CINETEAM COMMERCIALS B.V. (PAGE 203)

BEST FAR EASTERN LETTERHEAD
ART DIRECTOR: ZEMPAKU SUZUKI
CLIENT: CONTEMPORARY JEWELRY GALLERY YU (PAGE 57)

HONORABLE MENTION
ART DIRECTOR: SPENCER WALTERS
CLIENT: COMPUTER REPAIR (PAGE 49)

COMMENTARY BY JOE DUFFY

PORTRAIT BY KEVIN PETERSON, PARALLEL PRODUCTIONS

The Importance of Being Different

There is something wonderful about receiving a great letter, especially these days, when letter writing is rare. Perhaps it's rare because most people no longer have the time to think through the complicated process of self-expression. Or maybe it's just too difficult to attempt to cut through the piles of junk that find their way to our mailboxes. I think it also has a lot to do with that vulnerable feeling many of us get when committing our thoughts a printed page. □ Whatever the reasons, writing a letter provides one of the most genuine opportunities to stand out in a world of depersonalized communication. Whether it's a personal letter to an old friend or a critical business letter to a trusted client, with technology and the advancing state of communication arts it ought to be easier than ever to make a recipient sit up and take notice. And while I go along with the notion that the contents of our letters can't be overpowered by their forms — how about everyone stepping back, applying some perspective and lightening up a little when it comes to making judgments about how these letters ought to be clothed? □ This is about character, after all. □ I'm personally sick to death of hearing the obsessively buttoned-up corporate world lecture us at holy length about their need to avoid risk in their graphic identities. It's not risk they fear; it's the appearance of risk. By avoiding such appearances, the real risks to identity (such as the lack of any) fail to be assessed and intelligently managed. And nowhere in the world are these champions of grayness, conformity, and stiffness more effective in stifling individualism and uniqueness than in the category of business stationery. □ In the US in particular, where communication is becoming the fastest growing form of business and its largest export, the grind towards sameness seems really dumb. Even media companies and ad agencies, who consider themselves among the last great bastions of "cre-

ativity," insist that their identities must be mere frames for the real creativity which is their product. □ Well, come on. Every letter we write is a product, and therefore ought to be a true expression of the company or person who's writing it. And an integral part of every product is its package. Why on earth wouldn't every company that feels it is special and unique not want to express that uniqueness in all its communications? Why don't more of the allegedly different companies in our modern corporate world want to stand out? How can imitation be mistaken as an asset in such a competitive environment? Don't the communication companies — even the good ones — care that the letters they send to clients all look the same and express as much brand personality as a law partnership or accounting firm? Have communication companies come to the point where they emulate accounting and law firms? □ Something is wrong with this picture. And we're in it. □ While I haven't seen the finished project, history tells me this volume will no doubt be filled with excellent examples of truly expressive letterheads from a wide range of companies. □ The designers represented here are an incredibly diverse group in terms of age, size of firm, client lists, personal aesthetic, background, type of client relationship, budget parameters, and so on. The clients showcased on the following pages are every bit as eclectic. What makes a publication like this so great is the fact that it is almost all-inclusive. Almost.The ones you will not find included are the ones which need it most: the Fortune 500 companies, their ad agencies and design firms. These are the companies which have the greatest opportunity of reaching the largest audience. In so doing, they could help take design to its highest level. □ Companies are people. People who express themselves well are more successful than those who don't. □ It's that simple ■

Einen Brief zu bekommen ist etwas Wunderbares, besonders heute, wo das Briefeschreiben rar geworden ist. □ Vielleicht ist das so, weil die meisten Leute nicht mehr die Zeit haben, nachzudenken und ihre Gedanken zu formulieren. Oder vielleicht erscheint es aussichtslos, sich mit einem Brief gegen die Berge von Junk Mail, die in unseren Briefkästen landen, durchzusetzen. □ Ich glaube, es hat auch mit dem seltsamen Gefühl von Verletzlichkeit zu tun, das uns überfällt, wenn wir unsere Gedanken so unauslöschlich niederschreiben. □ Was immer die Gründe, das Schreiben eines Briefes gibt uns eine echte Gelegenheit, uns in einer Welt entpersönlichter Kommunikation abzuheben. Ob es sich um einen Brief an einen alten Freund handelt oder um einen schwierigen Geschäftsbrief an einen guten Kunden, es sollte (angesichts der Technologie und der fortschrittlichen Art der

Kommunikation) leichter denn je sein, den Empfänger dazu zu bringen, sich hinzusetzen und den Brief zu lesen. Ich gebe zwar zu, dass der Inhalt unserer Briefe nicht von ihrer Form übertroffen werden kann, aber wie wäre es, wenn jeder einen Schritt zurücktreten würde, um den richtigen Abstand und einen klaren Blick zu bekommen, wenn es zu beurteilen gilt, welche Aufmachung für solche Briefe geeignet wäre. □ Das ist schliesslich eine Frage des Charakters. □ Mich persönlich macht es krank, mir von total zugeknöpften Geschäftsleuten endlose Vorträge anhören zu müssen, warum sie bei ihrem graphischen Auftritt kein Risiko eingehen dürfen. Sie haben gar keine Angst vor dem Risiko, es geht um den Anschein von Risiko. Indem man diesen Anschein zu vermeiden sucht, verhindert man, dass die wirklichen Risiken (wie ihr Nichtvorhandensein)

JOE DUFFY IS THE PRESIDENT/CREATIVE DIRECTOR OF JOE DUFFY DESIGN IN MINNEAPOLIS AND NEW YORK. DUFFY DESIGN HAS DONE AWARD WINNING BRAND IDENTITY WORK FOR A LONG LIST OF CLIENTS INCLUDING THE COCA-COLA COMPANY, JIM BEAM BRANDS, LEE JEANS, AND THE STROH BREWERY COMPANY. JOE HAS BEEN A NATIONAL BOARD MEMBER OF THE AMERICAN INSTITUTE OF GRAPHIC ARTS AND HAS LECTURED ON DESIGN THROUGHOUT THE U.S., EUROPE AND AUSTRALIA.

nicht ermessen und intelligent gehandhabt werden können. Und nirgends, wirklich nirgends verhindern diese Meister der Eintönigkeit und Steifheit Persönlichkeit und Einzigartigkeit erfolgreicher als im Bereich der Firmenbriefschaften. □ Besonders in den USA, wo Kommunikation der am schnellsten wachsende Wirtschaftszweig und wichtigster Exportartikel ist, ist das Streben nach Gleichförmigkeit wirklich dumm. Selbst Mediafirmen und Werbeagenturen, die sich selbst für die letzten grossen Bastionen der «Kreativität» halten, stehen auf dem Standpunkt, dass ihr visueller Auftritt nur der Rahmen für die wirkliche Kreativität zu sein hat – ihr Produkt bzw. ihre Dienstleistung. □ Dabei ist jeder Brief, den wir schreiben, ein Produkt, und er sollte deshalb Ausdruck der Firma oder Person sein, die ihn schreibt. Zu einem Produkt gehört auch seine Verpackung (ein Thema, auf das ich mich hier besser nicht einlasse). Warum sollte nicht jede Firma, die sich für speziell und einzigartig hält, den Wunsch haben, diese Einzigartigkeit in allen ihren Kommunikations-mitteln zum Ausdruck zu bringen? Warum wollen nicht mehr der angeblich so besonderen Firmen in unserer modernen Geschäftswelt aus der Masse herausragen? Wie kann man Imitation bei einer so harten Konkurrenzsituation als Vorteil betrachten? Macht es den Kommunikationsfirmen – sogar den guten – nichts aus, wenn die Briefe, die sie an potentielle Kunden schicken, alle gleich aussehen

und so viel Persönlichkeit ausstrahlen wie eine Anwaltskanzlei oder ein Steuerberatungsbüro? Sind die Kommunikationsfirmen an einem Punkt angelangt, an dem sie Steuer- und Anwaltsbüros nacheifern wollen? □ An diesem Bild stimmt etwas nicht. Und wir stecken mitten drin. □ Während ich diesen Text schreibe, liegt mir *Graphis Letterhead 3* zwar noch nicht vor, aber erfahrungsgemäss wird es zweifellos hervorragende Beispiele wirklich ausdrucksstarker Briefköpfe von einem breiten Spektrum von Firmen enthalten. □ Die hier vorgestellten Designer sind hinsichtlich Alter, Firmengrösse, Kundenliste, persönlicher Auffassung von Ästhetik, Ausbildung, der Art ihrer Kundenbeziehungen, Budgets etc. etc. eine unglaublich un-terschiedliche Gruppe. Genau so eklektisch sind die Arbeiten und damit auch die Kunden, die auf den folgenden Seiten vorgestellt werden. Was eine Publikation wie diese so grossartig macht, ist die Tatsache, dass hier fast alles vertreten ist. Fast. □ Was man nicht entdecken wird sind Firmen, die es am nötigsten hätten: Die 500 erfolgreichsten Firmen, die auf der Liste der Zeitschrift *Fortune* fi-gurieren. Auch ihre Agenturen und Designbüros fehlen. Dabei hätten sie die besten Voraussetzungen, das grösste Publikum anzusprechen und sie könnten dazu beitragen, die Qualität im Design optimal zu fördern. □ Firmen sind Leute. Leute, die sich gut ausdrücken, sind erfolgreicher als die, die das nicht tun. □ So einfach ist das. ■

. . . .

Quel sentiment merveilleux que de recevoir une lettre, particulièrement aujourd'hui où la correspondance est tombée en désuétude. □ Peut-être est-ce parce que le temps nous manque, le temps de mener une réflexion approfondie, de se laisser entraîner dans les arcanes de sa pensée et de la coucher sur le papier. Ou peut-être nous paraît-il vain de rivaliser avec ces piles de prospectus bariolés, de publipostages et autres publicités qui nous envahissent au quotidien? □ Pour ma part, je crois que c'est en partie parce que nous ressentons un curieux sentiment de vulnérabilité à figer nos pensées pour l'éternité. □ Quelles qu'en soient les raisons, écrire une lettre nous donne une occasion unique de nous élever au-dessus du monde de la communication standard, impersonnelle. Qu'il s'agisse d'une lettre à un vieil ami, d'une lettre délicate adressée à un client important, les moyens de communication sophistiqués dont nous disposons à l'heure actuelle devraient nous permettre – aujourd'hui plus que jamais – d'amener le destinataire à prendre le temps de lire le message. Certes, j'en conviens, la présentation d'une lettre ne saurait dépasser son contenu, mais ne serait-il pas opportun de prendre un peu de recul et de nous demander comment l'habiller? □ Après tout, c'est une question de caractère. □ S'il y a bien une chose que je ne supporte plus, c'est d'entendre tous ces hommes d'affaires dans leur complet-veston couleur muraille nous expliquer en long et large pourquoi ils ne peuvent se permettre d'encourir le moindre

risque en matière de présentation graphique. En fait, ce n'est pas du risque qu'ils ont peur, mais de l'idée même du risque. Et c'est justement cette attitude qui les empêche de cerner les vrais risques (ou leur absence) et d'y apporter des solutions intelligentes. Dans aucun autre domaine que celui de la correspondance commerciale, je dis bien aucun autre, ces virtuoses de la monotonie, de la rigidité, de la grisaille ne se font fort d'étouffer dans l'œuf avec autant de « brio » tout signe de personnalité et d'originalité. □ Aux Etats-Unis plus qu'ailleurs, où la communication connaît une expansion fulgurante et est en train de devenir le premier produit d'exportation, cette quête quasi maladive de l'uniformisation est d'une rare ineptie. Même les sociétés spécialisées dans la communication et les agences de publicité, qui se targuent d'être les derniers bastions de la créativité, estiment que leur identité graphique doit se réduire à un élément-cadre servant leur véritable créativité, soit le produit ou les prestations qu'ils vendent. □ Mais que diable! Chaque lettre que nous écrivons n'est-elle pas un produit? Ne doit-elle pas être l'expression fidèle de l'entreprise ou de la personne qui l'a rédigée? Et tout produit ne mérite-t-il pas un emballage digne de ce nom? (Je préfère ne pas aborder ce sujet ici!) Pourquoi une société qui est fermement convaincue de sa spécificité ne devrait-elle pas exprimer sa différence à travers tous les moyens de communication dont elle dispose? Pourquoi n'y a-t-il pas plus d'entreprises dans le monde

. . . .

JOE DUFFY IST LEITER UND CREATIVE DIRECTOR VON JOE DUFFY DESIGN IN MINNEAPOLIS UND NEW YORK. DUFFY DESIGNS MARKENIDEN-TITÄTS-PROGRAMME FÜR KUNDEN WIE COCA-COLA, JIM BEAM, LEE JEANS UND THE STROH BREWERY WURDEN MIT ZAHLREICHEN PREISEN AUSGEZEICHNET. JOE IST IM VORSTAND DES AIGA UND HAT IN DEN USA, EUROPA UND AUSTRALIEN REFERATE ÜBER DESIGN GEHALTEN.

moderne des affaires qui, persuadées de leur «différence», manifestent le désir de sortir du lot, de marquer le coup? Comment peut-on voir dans la standardisation un atout alors que la concurrence fait rage? Les entreprises spécialisées dans la communication – même les bonnes – ne se rendent-elles donc pas compte que leurs lettres de démarchage sont aussi peu originales que celles d'un cabinet d'avocats ou de conseillers fiscaux? En seraient-elles arrivées au point de vouloir les imiter? □ A l'heure où j'écris ces lignes, je n'ai pas encore eu l'occasion de voir le présent volume, mais, par expérience, je sais qu'il contient des en-têtes alliant avec un égal bonheur originalité et expressivité, de vrais petits chefs-d'œuvre du genre, représentatifs d'un large éventail de sociétés et d'agences. □ Les graphistes sélectionnés pour cet ouvrage forment un ensemble des plus hétéroclites en termes d'âge, de taille de leur société, de formation, d'esthétique personnelle, de clientèle, de relations commerciales, de budgets, etc. – et témoignent de leur différence,

(PRECEDING PAGE) CLIENT: McCOOL DESIGN FIRM: JOE DUFFY DESIGN ART DIRECTOR: JOE DUFFY DESIGNER: JOE DUFFY ILLUSTRATOR: NANCY CARLSON COUNTRY: USA INDUSTRY: CHILDRENS BOOKS ■ (THIS PAGE AND OPPOSITE) CLIENT: MATT ESECSON DESIGN FIRM: JOE DUFFY DESIGN ART DIRECTOR: NEIL POWELL DESIGNER: NEIL POWELL ILLUSTRATOR: NEIL POWELL COUNTRY: USA INDUSTRY: PRODUCT DESIGN AND MARKETING

différence qui se reflète dans les travaux présentés au fil des pages suivantes. Ce qui fait la richesse d'un tel ouvrage, c'est qu'il représente presque tous les styles. Presque! □ Parmi les absents figurent les sociétés qui auraient le plus besoin de s'illustrer, à savoir les 500 sociétés répertoriées dans le magazine *Fortune* ainsi que leurs agences de publicité et de design. Celles qui auraient les moyens de toucher le plus large public et de contribuer ainsi à élever la qualité du design à son meilleur niveau. □ Toute société est constituée de personnes. Celles qui savent s'exprimer ont plus de chance de réussir que celles qui ne le font pas. □ C'est aussi simple que ça. ■

JOE DUFFY EST PRÉSIDENT ET DIRECTEUR ARTISTIQUE DE L'AGENCE JOE DUFFY DESIGN À MINNEAPOLIS ET À NEW YORK. LES IDENTITÉS DE MARQUES CRÉÉES PAR LUI POUR UNE LONGUE LIST DE CLIENTS PRESTIGIEUX – DONT COCA-COLA, JIM BEAM, LEE JEANS ET THE STROH BREWERY COMPNAY – LUI ONT VALU PLUSIEURS DISTINCTIONS. JOE EST MEMBRE DU COMITÉ NATIONAL DE L'AIGA ET A DONNÉ DE NOMBREUSES CONFÉRENCES SUR LE DESIGN AUX ETATS-UNIS, EN EUROPE ET EN AUSTRALIE.

(OPPOSITE) CLIENT: DONALD M. WARD DESIGN FIRM: BLACKBIRD CREATIVE ART DIRECTOR: PATRICK SHORT DESIGNER: PATRICK SHORT PHOTOGRAPHER: ALEX BEE COUNTRY: USA INDUSTRY: ACCOUNTANT/STEUERBERATER/SOCIÉTÉ FIDUCAIRE ■ (THIS PAGE) CLIENT: WORK (CABELL HARRIS) DESIGN FIRM: HALEY JOHNSON DESIGN CO. DESIGNERS: HALEY JOHNSON, DAN OLSON ILLUSTRATOR: HALEY JOHNSON COUNTRY: USA INDUSTRY: ADVERTISING AGENCY/WERBEAGENTUR/AGENCE DE PUBLICITÉ

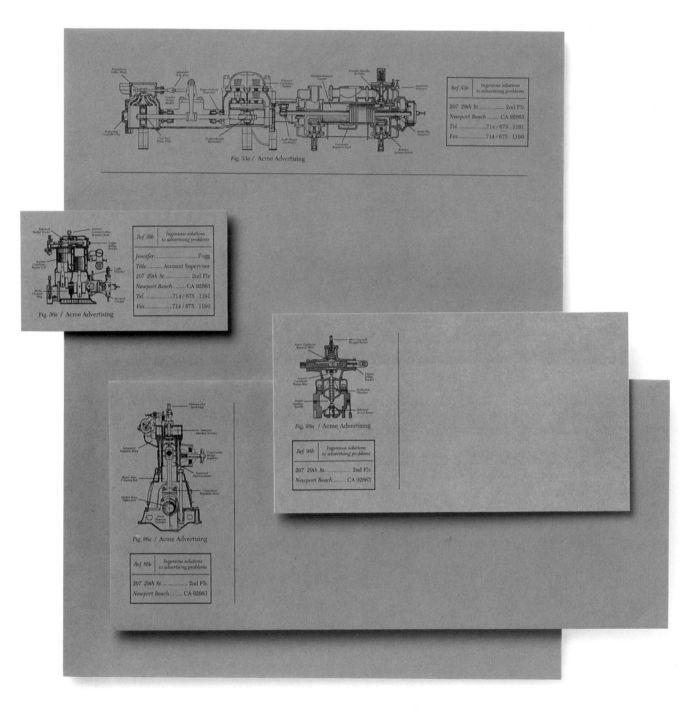

CLIENT: ACME ADVERTISING

DESIGN FIRM: ACME ADVERTISING

ART DIRECTOR/DESIGNER: SAKOL MONGKOLKASETARIN

PHOTOGRAPHER: PETER SAMUELS

ILLUSTRATOR: STOCK

COPYWRITER: BRIAN WEST

COUNTRY: USA

INDUSTRY: ADVERTISING AGENCY/WERBEAGENTUR/AGENCE DE PUBLICITÉ

CLIENT: HAGGMAN, INC.

DESIGN FIRM: HAGGMAN, INC.

ART DIRECTOR: AMY ELIZABETH FARR

ILLUSTRATOR: ROB DAY

COUNTRY: USA

INDUSTRY: ADVERTISING AGENCY/WERBEAGENTUR/AGENCE DE PUBLICITÉ

Prisoners of Advertising

The San Francisco Ad Club
150 Post street, Suite 325, San Francisco, California 94108
Telephone 415·986·3878 FAX 415·986·7457

CLIENT: SAN FRANCISCO AD CLUB
DESIGN FIRM: HAL RINEY & PARTNERS
ART DIRECTOR/DESIGNER: CHRIS CHAFFIN
ILLUSTRATOR: JOE SPENCER
COUNTRY: USA
INDUSTRY: ADVERTISING ASSOCIATION/CLUB/WERBE-CLUB/ASSOCIATION DE PUBLICITÉ

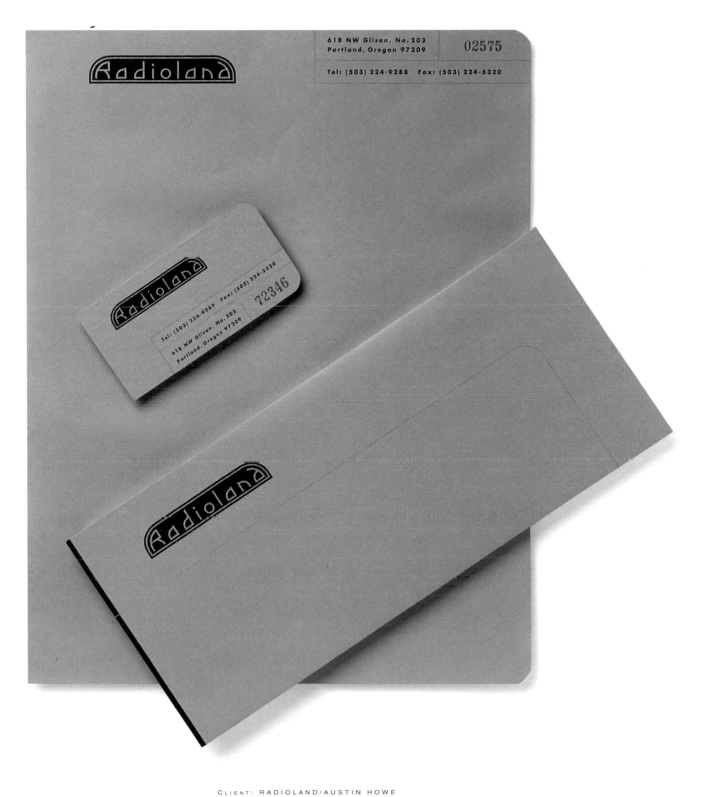

Client: RADIOLAND/AUSTIN HOWE
Design Firm: SANDSTROM DESIGN
Art Director/Designer: STEVEN SANDSTROM
Illustrator: DONJIRO BAN
Country: USA
Industry: RADIO ADVERTISING, CREATIVE AND PRODUCTION/RADIO-WERBUNG, HERSTELLUNG UND
PRODUKTION/PRODUCTION ET RÉALISATION DE LA PUBLICITÉ RADIO

CLIENT: MONNIER, GENINASCA, DELEFORTRIE
DESIGN FIRM: LES ATELIERS A (DE WAVRE)
ART DIRECTOR/DESIGNER: MICHELE GROSSENBACHER
COUNTRY: SWITZERLAND
INDUSTRY: ARCHITECTS/ARCHITEKTURBÜRO/BUREAU D'ARCHITECTES

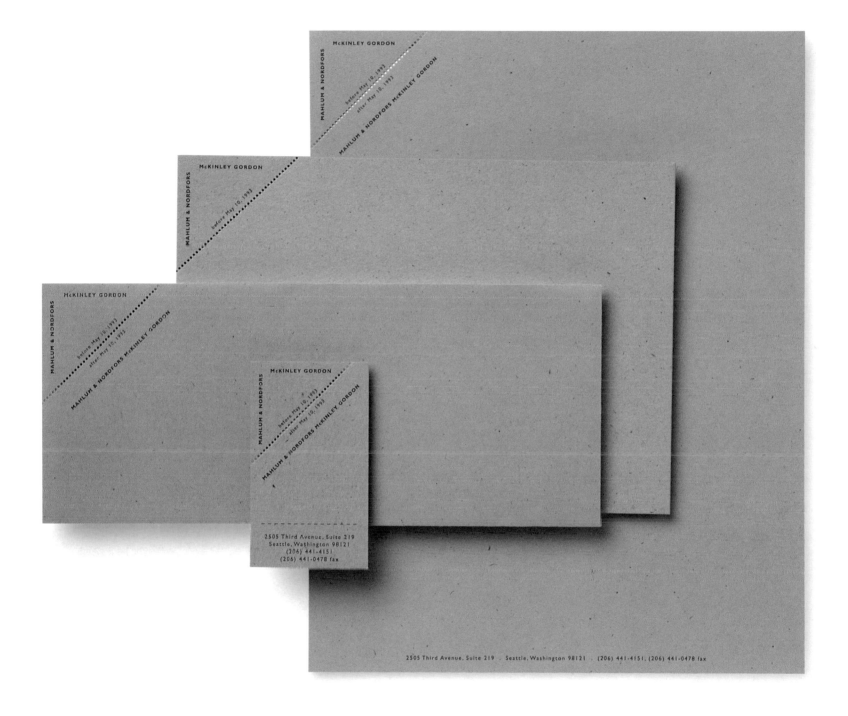

CLIENT: MAHLUM & NORDFORS MCKINLEY GORDON
DESIGN FIRM: HORNALL ANDERSON DESIGN WORKS, INC.
ART DIRECTOR: JACK ANDERSON
DESIGNERS: JACK ANDERSON, SCOTT EGGERS, LEO RAYMUNDO
COUNTRY: USA
INDUSTRY: ARCHITECTS/ARCHITEKTURBÜRO/BUREAU D'ARCHITECTES

Client: DESTON ENTERTAINMENT

Designer: COMARK GROUP

Printer: BURDGE, INC.

Country: USA

Industry: ARTISTS' REPRESENTATIVE/KÜNSTLERAGENTUR/AGENCE ARTISTIQUE

CLIENT: JANE JENNI

DESIGN FIRM: HALEY JOHNSON DESIGN CO.

DESIGNER/ILLUSTRATOR: HALEY JOHNSON

PHOTOGRAPHER: GEORGE PEER

COUNTRY: USA

INDUSTRY: ART REPRESENTATIVE/KUNSTAGENTUR/AGENCE D'ART

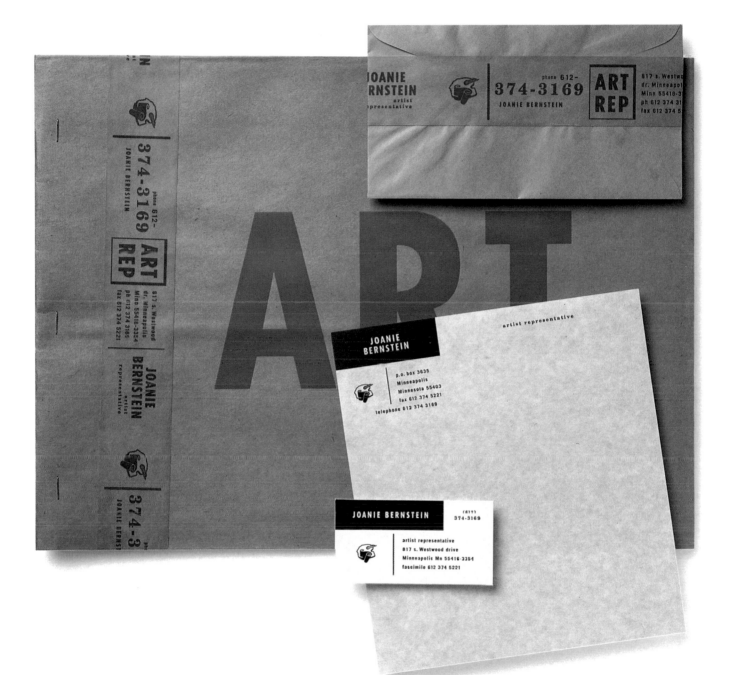

CLIENT: JOANIE BERNSTEIN

DESIGN FIRM: WERNER DESIGN WERKS INC.

ART DIRECTOR/DESIGNER/ILLUSTRATOR: SHARON WERNER

COUNTRY: USA

INDUSTRY: ARTISTS' REPRESENTATIVE/KÜNSTLERAGENTUR/AGENCE ARTISTIQUE

(ABOVE) CLIENT: FREEMAN WHITEHURST DESIGN FIRM: CFD DESIGN DESIGNER: STEVE DITKO COUNTRY: USA INDUSTRY: ARTISTS' REPRESENTATIVE/KÜNSTLERAGENTUR/AGENCE ARTISTIQUE ■ (OPPOSITE) CLIENT: SATISFAC CREDIT UNION DESIGN FIRM: TUCKER DESIGN ART DIRECTOR: BARRIE TUCKER DESIGNER/ILLUSTRATOR: HANS KOHLA COUNTRY: AUSTRALIA INDUSTRY: BANK/BANQUE

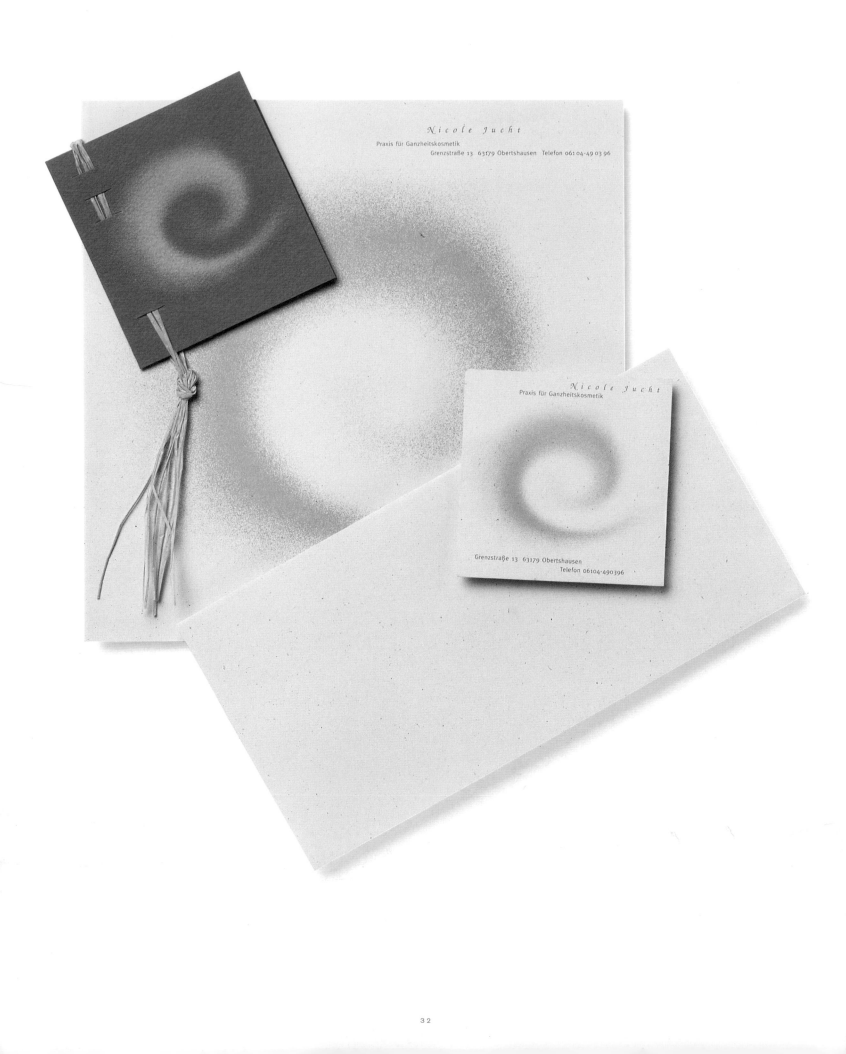

rent-a-van, inc.
Qualico Motor Sales

400 South 9th Street
Lincoln, NE 68508
(402) 476-2678

rent-a-van, inc.
Qualico Motor Sales

400 South 9th Street
Lincoln, NE 68508
(402) 476-2678

Doug Tenney
General Manager

rent-a-van, inc.
Qualico Motor Sales

400 South 9th Street
Lincoln, NE 68508

(OPPOSITE PAGE) CLIENT: NICOLE JUCHT DESIGN FIRM: DREWS DESIGN ART DIRECTOR: BURGLIND DREWS DESIGNER: MECHTHILD STRIEFLER ILLUSTRATOR: ROBERT AREND COUNTRY: GERMANY INDUSTRY: BEAUTY SALON/KOSMETIKSTUDIO/SALON DE BEAUTÉ ■ (THIS PAGE) CLIENT: RENT-A-VAN, INC. DESIGN FIRM: THE LARSON GROUP ART DIRECTOR: KEITH CHRISTIANSON DESIGNER: KEITH CHRISTIANSON COUNTRY: USA INDUSTRY: CAR RENTAL/AUTOVERMIETUNG/LOCATION DE VOITURES

1260 NORTH BROAD STREET   HILLSIDE NEW JERSEY 07205   PHONE 908-353-1644 FAX 908-353-1644

RUBBER DUCK
CAR WASH
1260 NORTH BROAD STREET
HILLSIDE NEW JERSEY
07205

1260 NORTH BROAD STREET
HILLSIDE NEW JERSEY 07205
PHONE 908-353-1644
FAX 908-353-1644

RUBBER DUCK
CAR WASH

RUBBER DUCK
CAR WASH

CLIENT: RUBBER DUCK CAR WASH
DESIGN FIRM: PISARKIEWICZ & CO., INC.
ART DIRECTOR: MARY F. PISARKIEWICZ
DESIGNER: JENNIFER HARENBERG
COUNTRY: USA
INDUSTRY: CAR WASH/AUTOWASCHANLAGE/STATION DE LAVAGE

CLIENT: FÖLSER + SCHERNHUBER

DESIGN FIRM: FÖLSER + SCHERNHUBER

ART DIRECTOR/DESIGNER: PETER SCHMID

COUNTRY: AUSTRIA

INDUSTRY: COMMUNICATIONS/MARKETING

Linda J. Holland

Strategic

Marketing

Communications

Linda J. Holland

Strategic Marketing

Communications

1009 Urban Avenue

Durham, NC 27701

1009 Urban Avenue

Durham, NC 27701

919-682-4039

fax:919-682-4135

Linda J. Holland
Strategic Marketing Communications

1009 Urban Avenue, Durham, NC 27701
919-682-4039 fax:919-682-4135

CLIENT: LINDA HOLLAND
DESIGN FIRM: FGI ADVERTISING & DESIGN
ART DIRECTOR/DESIGNER/ILLUSTRATOR: RICK BAPTIST
COUNTRY: USA
INDUSTRY: COMMUNICATIONS/MARKETING

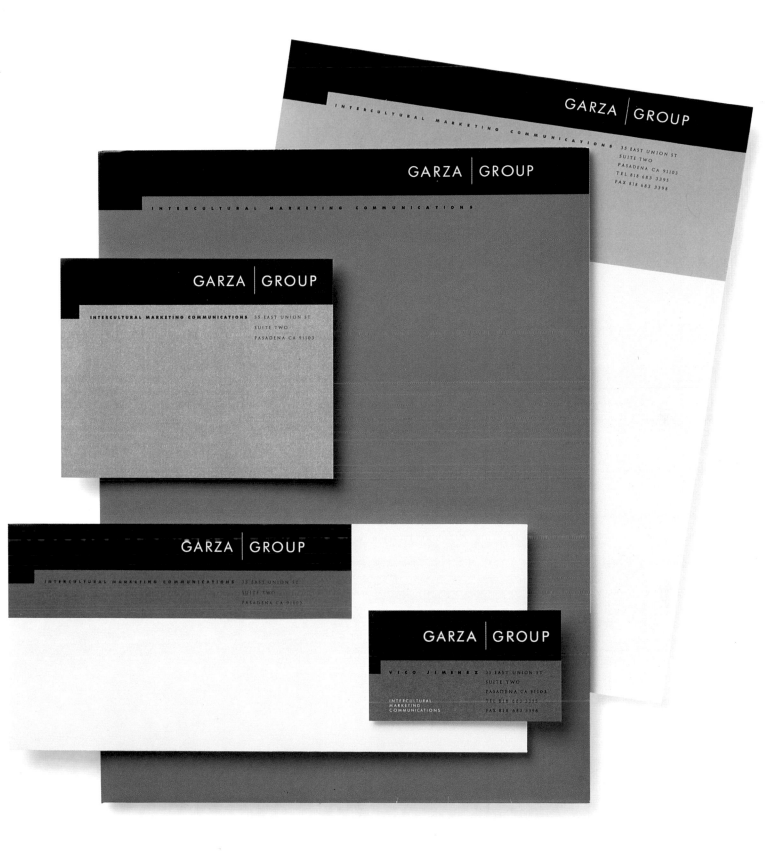

CLIENT: GARZA
DESIGN FIRM: GARZA GROUP COMMUNICATIONS
ART DIRECTOR/DESIGNER: AGUSTIN GARZA
COUNTRY: USA
INDUSTRY: MARKETING

Client: FAST BREAK COMMUNICATIONS
Design Firm: NEO-GEO OY
Art Director/Designer/Illustrator: EERO HEIKKINEN
Country: FINLAND
Industry: COMMUNICATIONS/KOMMUNIKATION

INFOFusion

Revolutionary institutional research methods
Rigorous audience identification and classification
Targeted copy, graphic design, and photography
Budget-sensitive print communications
Result-oriented distribution strategies
Exit analysis and product evaluation

1
Robert Topor
280 Easy Street
Suite 114
Mountain View, CA 94043-3736

2
Ann Granning Bennett
10634 Southwest Hedlund Avenue
Suite 193
Portland, OR 97219-7916

3
Bryan Peterson
2200 North Lamar Street
Suite 310
Dallas, TX 75202-1073

INFOFusion

1
Ann Granning Bennett
10634 Southwest Hedlund Avenue
Suite 193
Portland, OR 97219-7916

Call Ann at 503 635-6462

CLIENT: INFOFUSION

DESIGN FIRM: PETERSON & COMPANY

ART DIRECTOR/DESIGNER: BRYAN L. PETERSON

COUNTRY: USA

INDUSTRY: COMMUNICATIONS/MARKETING

EBERHARD WEBER

WEBER & WEBER
MANAGEMENT FÜR STRATEGIE & IMAGE
FAUNASTR. 59 40239 DÜSSELDORF
TELEFON 0211 6913 913 FAX 6913 118

WEBER & WEBER
MANAGEMENT FÜR STRATEGIE & IMAGE
FAUNASTR. 59 40239 DÜSSELDORF
TELEFON 0211 6913 913 FAX 6913 118

WEBER & WEBER
MANAGEMENT FÜR STRATEGIE & IMAGE
FAUNASTR. 59 40239 DÜSSELDORF
TELEFON 0211 6913 913 FAX 6913 118

WEBER & WEBER
MANAGEMENT FÜR STRATEGIE & IMAGE
FAUNASTR. 59 40239 DÜSSELDORF TELEFON 0211 6913 913 FAX 6913 118
KONTO 870 887 019 BANKLEITZAHL 301 602 13 DÜSSELDORFER BANK

Client: WEBER & WEBER
Art Directors: UTE KARABULUT, CLAUDIA SCHAPER
Country: GERMANY
Industry: STRATEGY AND IMAGE MANAGEMENT/MANAGEMENT FÜR STRATEGIE & IMAGE/CONSEIL EN STRATÉGIE ET IMAGE

CLIENT: KOHGA COMMUNICATION PRODUCTS INC.
DESIGN FIRM: BOLTS & NUTS STUDIO
ART DIRECTOR: KENZO NAKAGAWA
DESIGNERS: KENZO NAKAGAWA, HIROYASU NOBUYAMA, SATOSHI MORIKAMI
COUNTRY: JAPAN
INDUSTRY: COMMUNICATION AND ENTERTAINMENT ARTICLES/FUN-ARTIKEL ZUR KOMMUNIKATION UND
UNTERHALTUNG/ARTICLES DE 'FUN' DE COMMUNICATION ET DE DIVERTISSEMENT

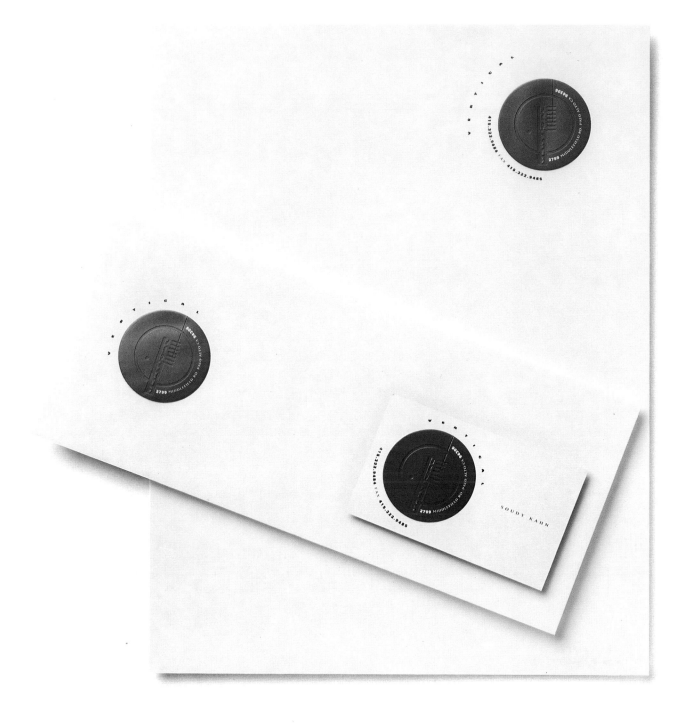

CLIENT: VERTICAL

DESIGN FIRM: TSANG, PROPP & GUERIN

ART DIRECTOR/DESIGNER: PAUL TSANG

COUNTRY: USA

INDUSTRY: MARKETING

CLIENT: VDR

DESIGN FIRM: IGREK

ART DIRECTOR/DESIGNER: NICOLAS BUSNEL

COUNTRY: FRANCE

INDUSTRY: CORPORATE IDENTITY CONSULTANTS/C.I.-BERATUNGSFIRMA/CONSEIL EN COMMUNICATION INTERNE, RELATIONS

PUBLIQUES ET COMMUNICATION INSTITUTIONNELLE

(THIS SPREAD)

CLIENT/DESIGN FIRM: F.G. BOES & PARTNER

ART DIRECTOR/DESIGNER: F.G. BOES

COUNTRY: SPAIN

INDUSTRY: COMMUNICATIONS/MARKETING

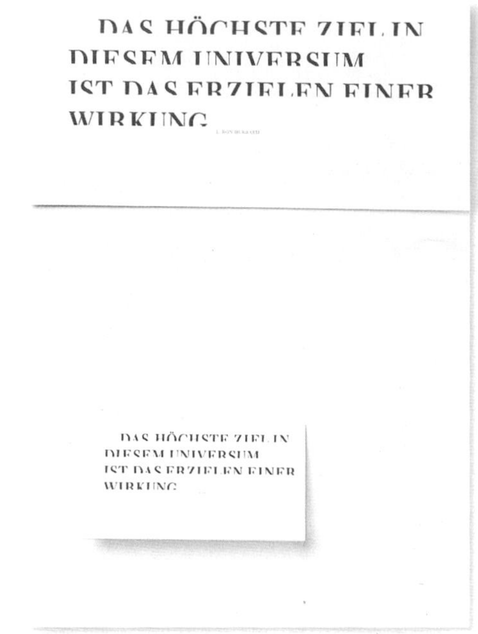

DAS HÖCHSTE ZIEL IN
DIESEM UNIVERSUM
IST DAS ERZIELEN EINER
WIRKUNG.

EINE GUTE IDEE MACHT SICH
SELBST IHREN MARKT.

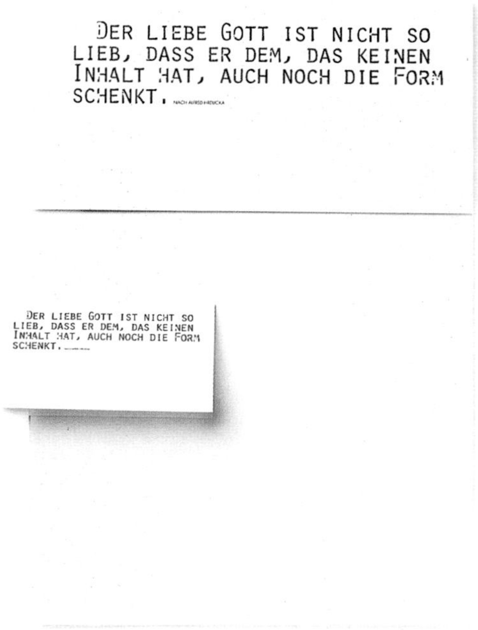

DER LIEBE GOTT IST NICHT SO
LIEB, DASS ER DEM, DAS KEINEN
INHALT HAT, AUCH NOCH DIE FORM
SCHENKT.

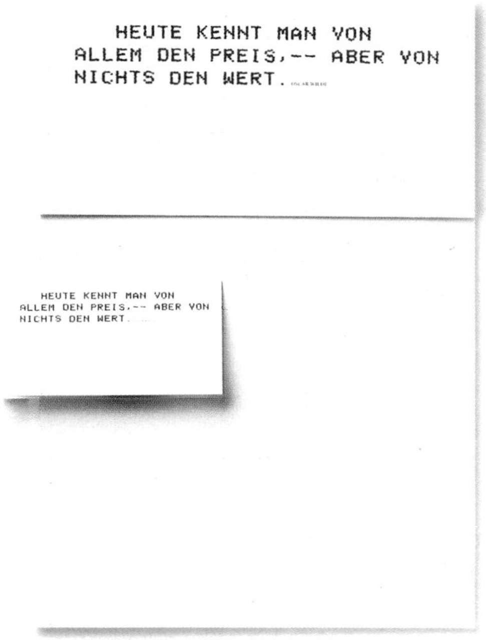

HEUTE KENNT MAN VON
ALLEM DEN PREIS,—— ABER VON
NICHTS DEN WERT.

DESIGN IST KUNST, DIE SICH NÜTZLICH MACHT. CARLOS OBERS

DESIGN IST KUNST,
DIE SICH NÜTZLICH
MACHT. CARLOS OBERS

(THIS SPREAD)

CLIENT/DESIGN FIRM: F.G. BOES & PARTNER

ART DIRECTOR/DESIGNER: F.G. BOES

COUNTRY: SPAIN

INDUSTRY: COMMUNICATIONS/MARKETING

CLIENT: MICROSOFT

DESIGN FIRM: THE LEONHARDT GROUP

DESIGNER: MARK POPICH

COUNTRY: USA

INDUSTRY: COMPUTER SOFTWARE

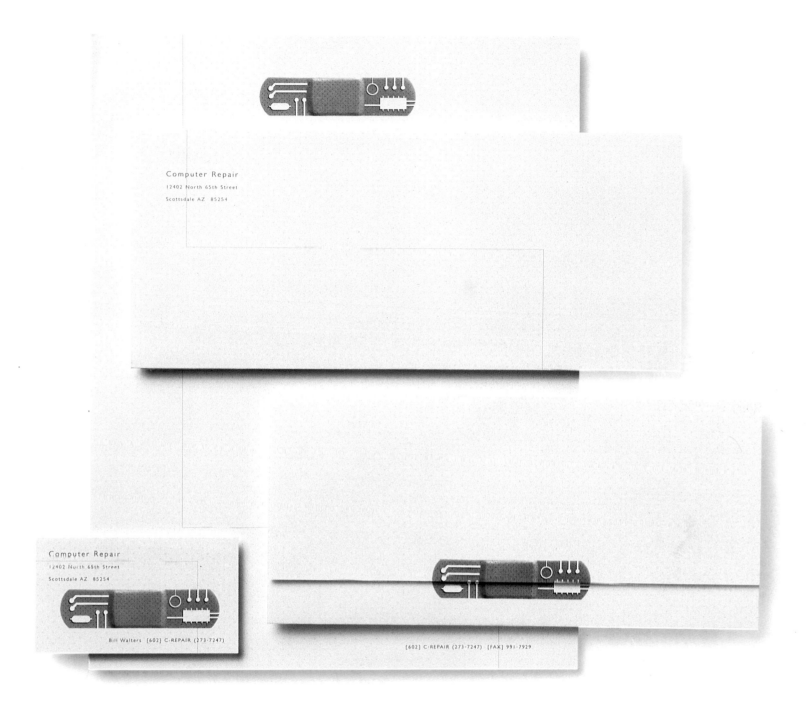

Computer Repair
12402 North 65th Street
Scottsdale AZ 85254

Computer Repair
12402 North 65th Street
Scottsdale AZ 85254

Bill Walters [602] C-REPAIR (273-7247)

[602] C-REPAIR (273-7247) [FAX] 991-7929

CLIENT: COMPUTER REPAIR
DESIGN FIRM: S.D. ZYNE
ART DIRECTOR/DESIGNER: SPENCER WALTERS
COUNTRY: USA
INDUSTRY: COMPUTER REPAIR/COMPUTERREPARATUR/
RÉPARATION D'ORDINATEURS

CLIENT: TENTH PLANET
DESIGN FIRM: GOODBY SILVERSTEIN + PARTNERS
ART DIRECTOR: PAUL CURTIN
DESIGNER: GEORGINA LEE
COUNTRY: USA
INDUSTRY: SOFTWARE DEVELOPMENT/ENTWICKLUNG VON SOFTWARE/DÉVELOPPEMENT DE LOGICIELS

E-Mail: info@goodnet.com
404 South Mill, Ste.C201
Tempe, Arizona 85281

GoodNet

David A. Pruett
pruett@goodnet.com
404 South Mill, Ste.C201
Tempe, Arizona 85281
Fax:602.303.0550
Tel:602.303.9500 #225

GoodNet

GoodNet

CLIENT: GOODNET

DESIGN FIRM/ART DIRECTOR/DESIGNER: AFTER HOURS CREATIVE

COUNTRY: USA

INDUSTRY: INTERNET ACCESS PROVIDER/INTERNET SERVICE/SERVICE INTERNET

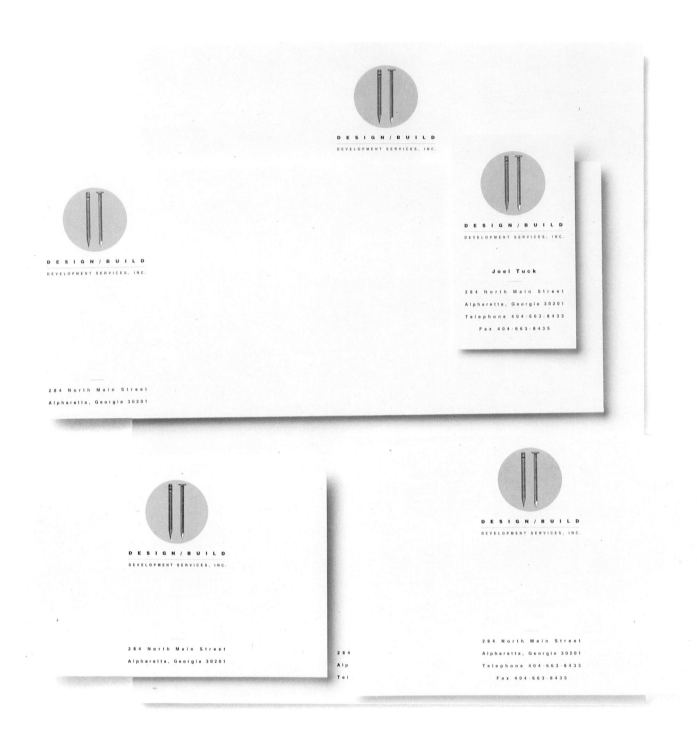

CLIENT: DESIGN/BUILD DEVELOPMENT SERVICES
DESIGN FIRM: DENNARD CREATIVE
ART DIRECTOR: BOB DENNARD
DESIGNER: JAMES LACEY
COUNTRY: USA
INDUSTRY: CONSTRUCTION/BAUWIRTSCHAFT

CLIENT: CLASSIC COMPANY

ART DIRECTOR/DESIGNER/ILLUSTRATOR: JOEL TEMPLIN

COUNTRY: USA

INDUSTRY: CONSTRUCTION/BAUWIRTSCHAFT

(ABOVE) CLIENT: OWEN WILLIAMS DESIGN FIRM: ROUNDEL DESIGN COMPANY ART DIRECTOR: MICHAEL DENNY DESIGNERS: JOHN BATESON, RACHAEL DINNIS, JONATHAN SIMPSON ILLUSTRATOR: TIM FLACH COUNTRY: GREAT BRITAIN INDUSTRY: CONSULTING ENGINEERS/BAUINGENIEURE/INGÉNIEURS-CONSEIL ■ (OPPOSITE) CLIENT: ASSOCIATION OF IDEAS LIMITED DESIGN FIRM: THE PARTNERS ART DIRECTOR: STEPHEN GIBBONS DESIGNERS: MARTIN MCLOUGHLIN, DAVID KIMPTON COUNTRY: GREAT BRITAIN INDUSTRY: ARCHITECTURE; EXHIBITION DESIGN/ARCHITEKTUR; MESSEBAU/ARCHITECTURE; STANDS DE FOIRES, SALONS D'EXPOSITION

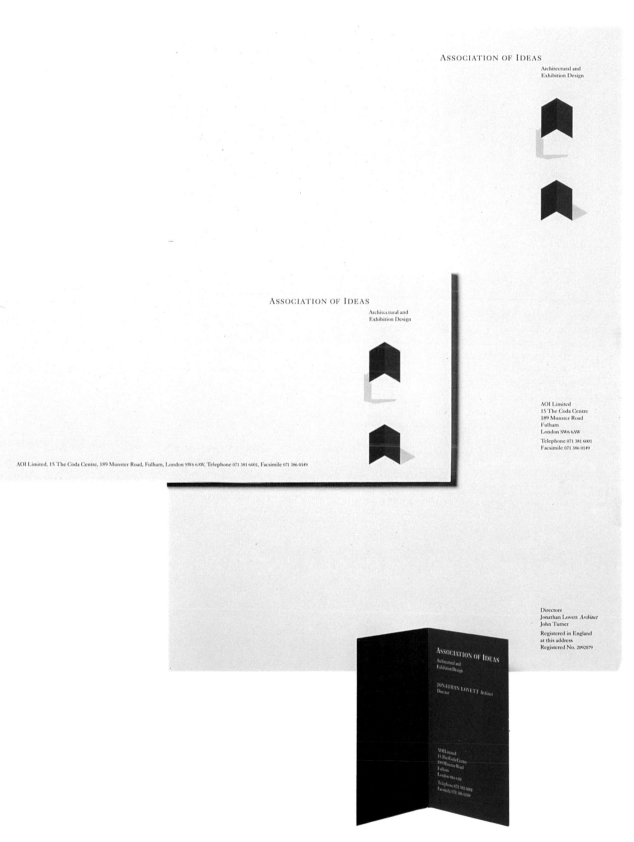

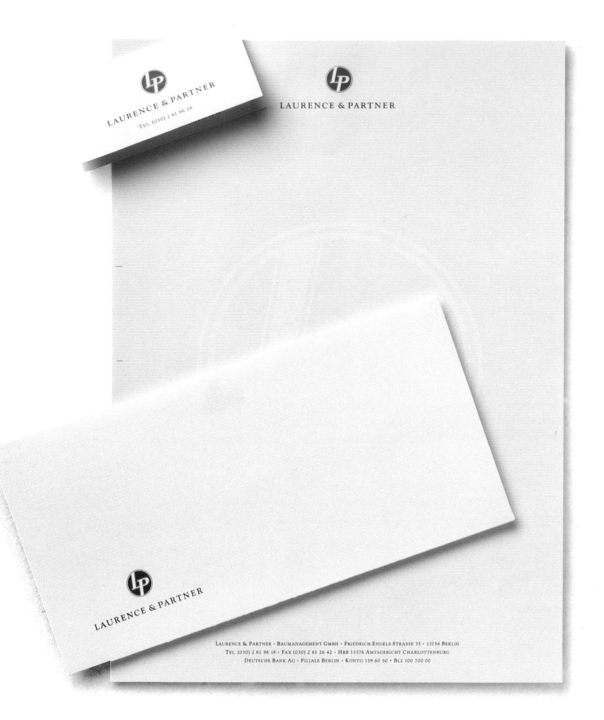

Client: LAURENCE & PARTNER
Design Firm: PEIX - GRAFIK & DESIGN
Designers: SVEN HERZBERG, KARSTEN RZEPKA
Country: GERMANY
Industry: CONSTRUCTION/BAUWIRTSCHAFT

CLIENT: CONTEMPORARY JEWELRY GALLERY YU
DESIGN FIRM: B-BI STUDIO INC.
ART DIRECTOR/DESIGNER: ZEMPAKU SUZUKI
PHOTOGRAPHER: TAMOTSU IKEDA
COUNTRY: JAPAN
INDUSTRY: JEWELRY/SCHMUCK/BIJOUTERIE

CLIENT: ALFONS MATHIS
DESIGN FIRM: FELDER GRAFIK DESIGN
ART DIRECTOR/DESIGNER: PETER FELDER
COUNTRY: AUSTRIA
INDUSTRY: TILER/FLIESENLEGER/CARRELEUR

CLIENT: FUCHS

ART DIRECTOR/DESIGNER: BERNHARD STRAUB

COUNTRY: GERMANY

INDUSTRY: CARPENTER/SCHREINEREI/MENUISERIE

CLIENT: DUFFY MINNEAPOLIS

DESIGN FIRM: DUFFY DESIGN

ART DIRECTOR/DESIGNER: NEIL POWELL

COUNTRY: USA

INDUSTRY: GRAPHIC DESIGN

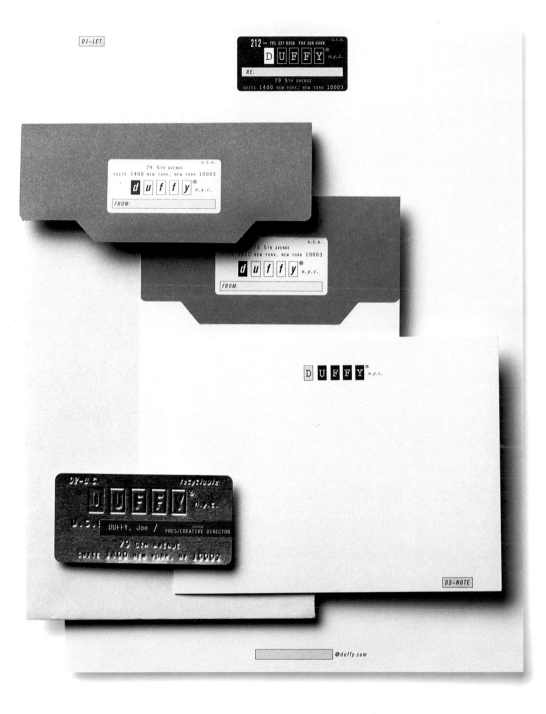

Client: DUFFY NEW YORK

Design Firm: DUFFY DESIGN

Art Director/Designer: NEIL POWELL

Country: USA

Industry: GRAPHIC DESIGN

CLIENT: HARD WERKEN TEN CATE BERGMANS DESIGN BV
DESIGN FIRM: CHARLES S. ANDERSON DESIGN COMPANY
ART DIRECTOR/DESIGNER: TODD PIPER-HAUSWIRTH
COUNTRY: NETHERLANDS
INDUSTRY: GRAPHIC DESIGN

MIRES DESIGN INC
2345 KETTNER BLVD SAN DIEGO CA 92101
PHONE: 619 234 6631 FAX: 619 234 1807

MIRES DESIGN INC.
2345 KETTNER BLVD SAN DIEGO CA 92101
PHONE: 619 234 6631 FAX: 619 234 1807
E MAIL: MIRES@MIRESDESIGN.COM

MIRES DESIGN INC
2345 KETTNER BOULEVARD
SAN DIEGO CALIFORNIA 92101

Client: MIRES DESIGN, INC.
Design Firm: MIRES DESIGN, INC.
Art Director/Designer: JOHN BALL
Letterpress: HAL TRUSCHKE
Country: USA
Industry: GRAPHIC DESIGN; MARKETING, COMMUNICATIONS

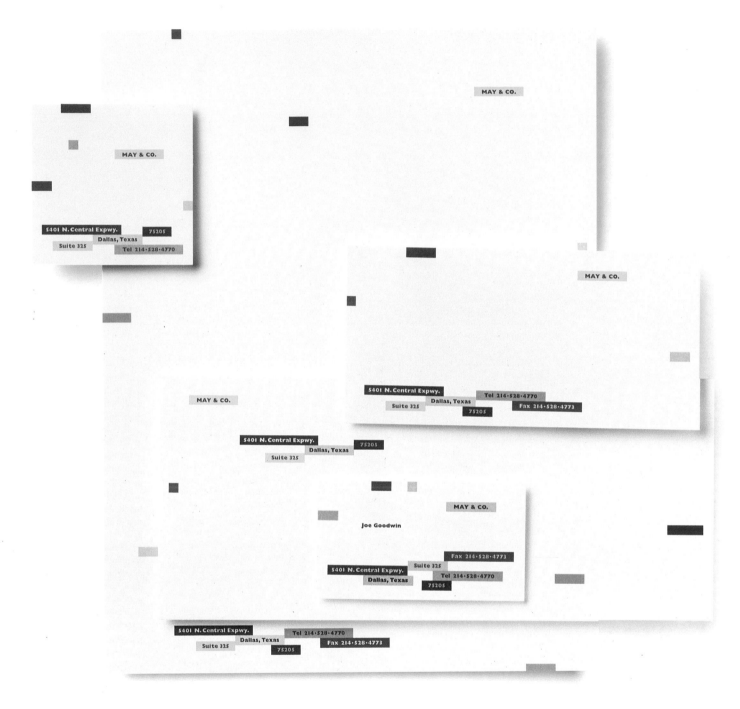

CLIENT: MAY & CO.

DESIGN FIRM: MAY & CO.

ART DIRECTOR: DOUGLAS MAY

DESIGNER: JO ORTIZ

COUNTRY: USA

INDUSTRY: GRAPHIC DESIGN; MARKETING, COMMUNICATIONS

Client: BRD DESIGN
Design Firm: BRD DESIGN .
Art Director/Designer: PETER KING ROBBINS
Photographer: GLEN ERLER
Country: USA
Industry: GRAPHIC DESIGN

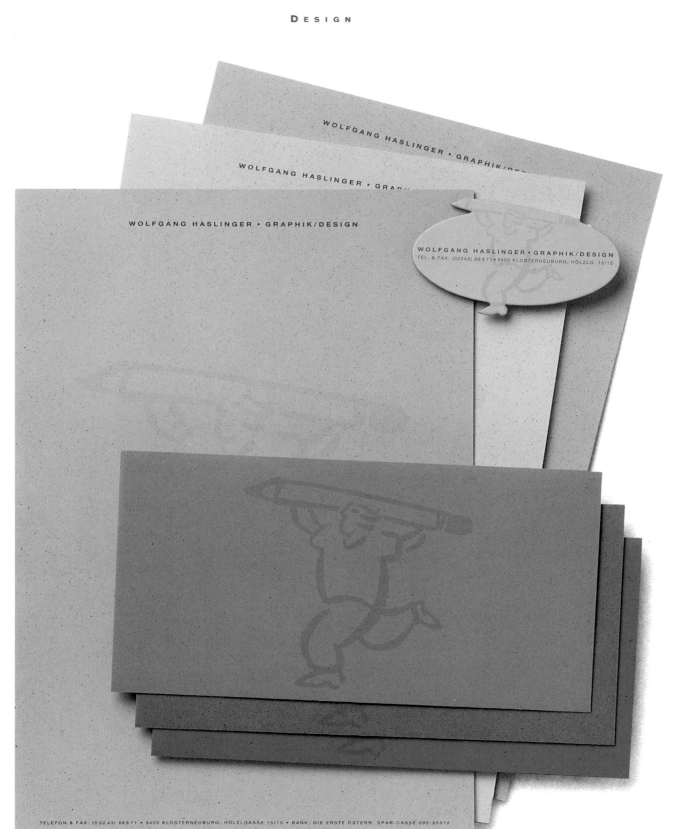

CLIENT: WOLFGANG HASLINGER GRAPHIK/DESIGN
DESIGN FIRM: WOLFGANG HASLINGER GRAPHIK/DESIGN
ART DIRECTOR/DESIGNER/ILLUSTRATOR: WOLFGANG HASLINGER
COUNTRY: AUSTRIA
INDUSTRY: GRAPHIC DESIGN

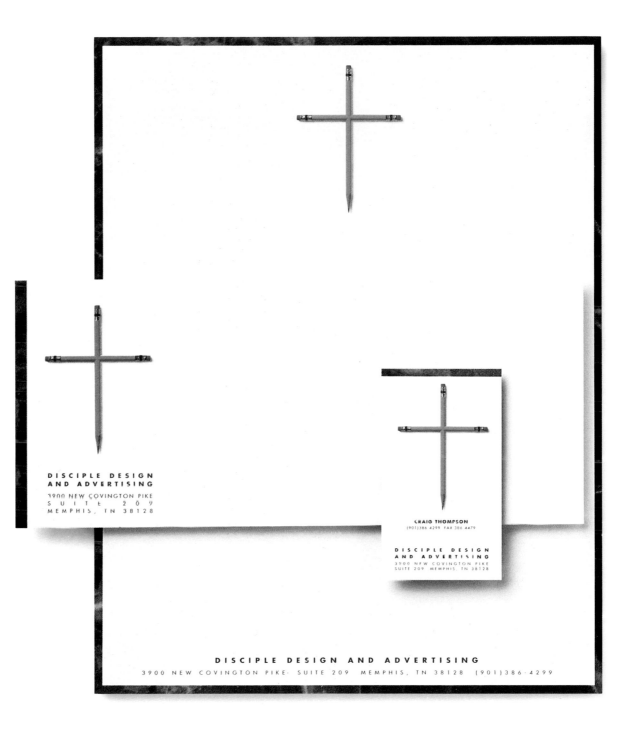

Client: DISCIPLE DESIGN AND ADVERTISING

Design Firm: DISCIPLE DESIGN AND ADVERTISING

Art Director/Designer: CRAIG THOMPSON

Photographer: PHILLIP PARKER

Country: USA

Industry: GRAPHIC DESIGN AND ADVERTISING/GRAPHIK-DESIGN UND WERBUNG/DESIGN GRAPHIQUE ET PUBLICITÉ

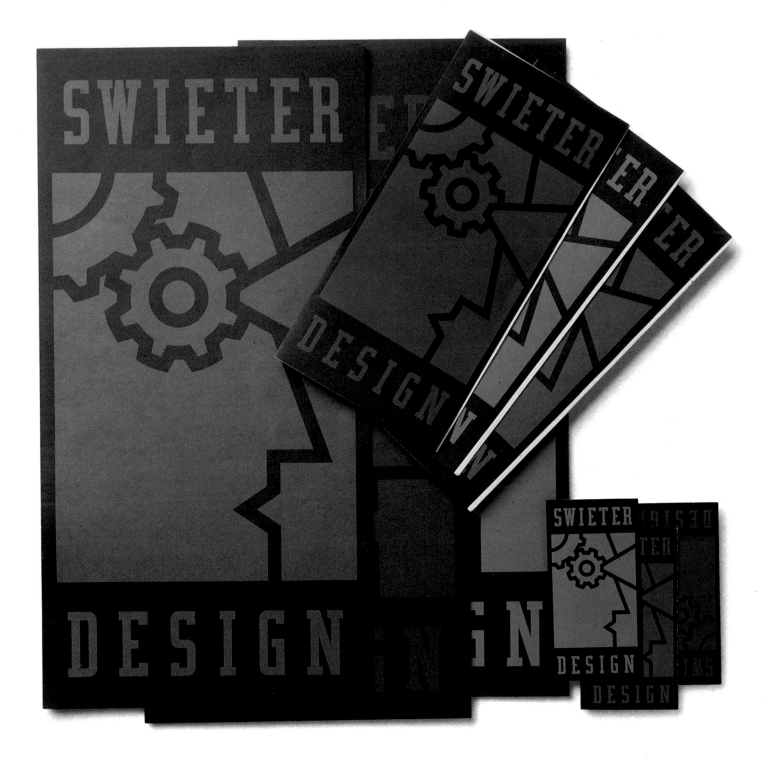

CLIENT: SWIETER DESIGN UNITED STATES

DESIGN FIRM: SWIETER DESIGN UNITED STATES

ART DIRECTOR/DESIGNER: JOHN SWIETER

COUNTRY: USA

INDUSTRY: GRAPHIC DESIGN

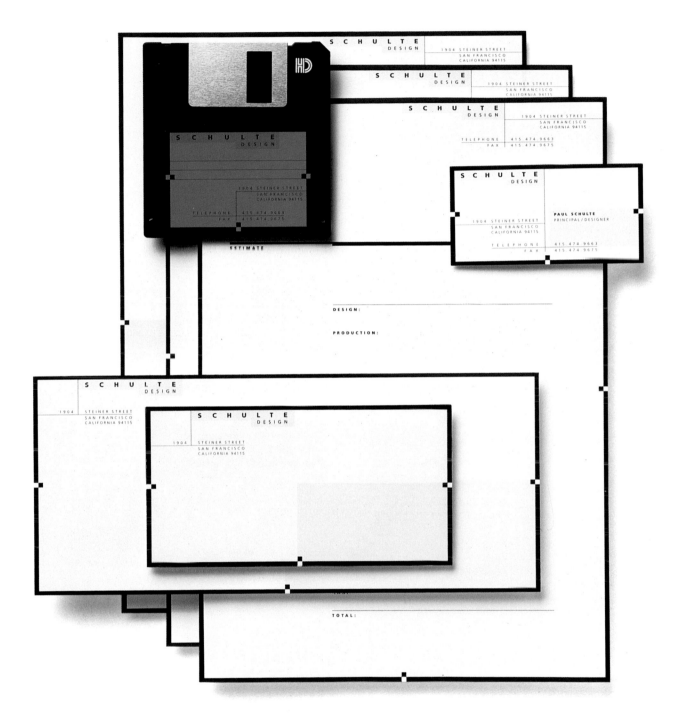

Client: SCHULTE DESIGN

Design Firm: SCHULTE DESIGN

Art Director/Designer: PAUL SCHULTE

Country: USA

Industry: GRAPHIC DESIGN

CLIENT: DEEP DESIGN
DESIGN FIRM: DEEP DESIGN
ART DIRECTORS: RICK GRIMSLEY, EDWARD JETT
DESIGNER: RICK GRIMSLEY
ILLUSTRATOR: MICHAEL SCHWAB
COUNTRY: USA
INDUSTRY: GRAPHIC DESIGN

CLIENT: MULLER + COMPANY
DESIGN FIRM: MULLER + COMPANY
ART DIRECTOR/DESIGNER: JOHN MULLER
COUNTRY: USA
INDUSTRY: GRAPHIC DESIGN

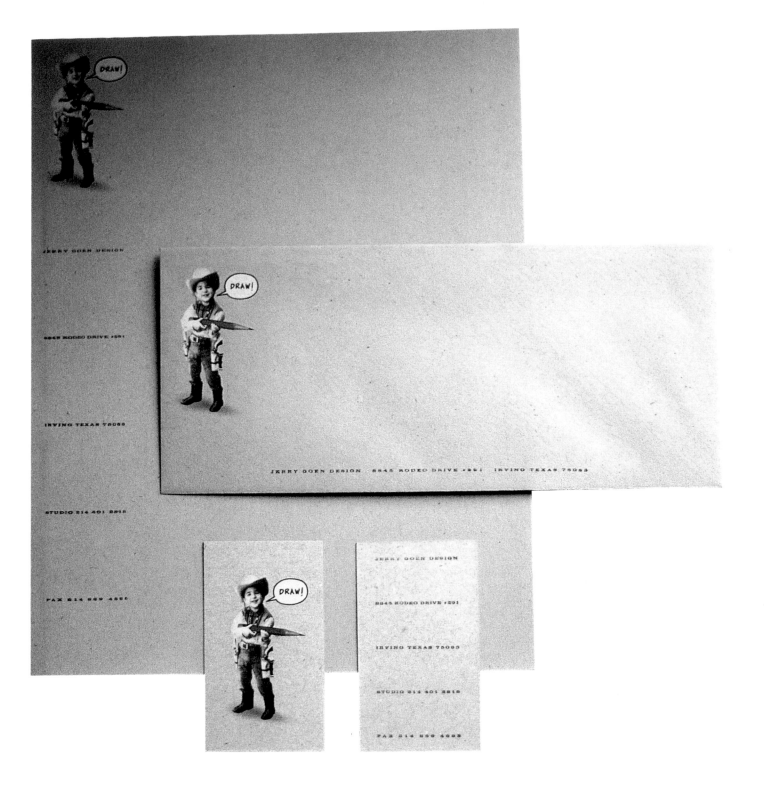

Client: JERRY GOEN DESIGN
Design Firm: JERRY GOEN DESIGN
Art Director/Designer: JERRY GOEN
Photographer: PATSY GOEN
Illustrator: MICHAEL MCMURTREY
Country: USA
Industry: GRAPHIC DESIGN

CLIENT: D. HILLER & PARTNER DESIGN GMBH

DESIGN FIRM: DESIGNEREI F. KOMMUNIKATION

ART DIRECTOR/DESIGNER: MATHIAS FORSTNER

COUNTRY: GERMANY

INDUSTRY: GRAPHIC DESIGN

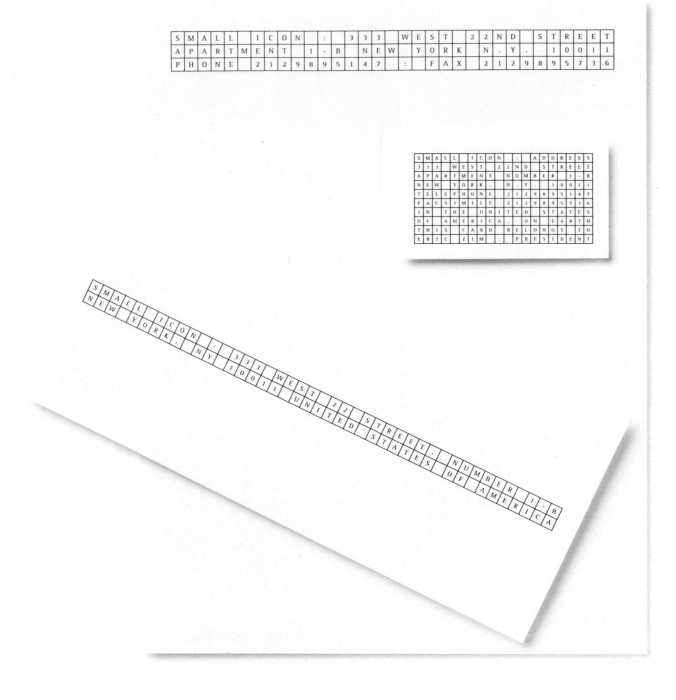

CLIENT: SMALL ICON

DESIGN FIRM: SMALL ICON

ART DIRECTOR/DESIGNER: ERIC ZIM

COUNTRY: USA

INDUSTRY: GRAPHIC DESIGN

AUSTRALIAN DESIGNER IN AMERICA
ANDREW CAWRSE 141B ASHBROOK
AVENUE TRINITY GARDENS 5068
SOUTH AUSTRALIA AUSTRALIA
CONTACT NUMBER +618 364 4985

CLIENT: ANDREW CAWRSE
ART DIRECTOR/DESIGNER: ANDREW CAWRSE
COUNTRY: USA
INDUSTRY: GRAPHIC DESIGN

CLIENT: SEGURA INC.

DESIGN FIRM: SEGURA INC.

ART DIRECTOR/DESIGNER: CARLOS SEGURA

PHOTOGRAPHER: GREG HECK

COUNTRY: USA

INDUSTRY: GRAPHIC DESIGN

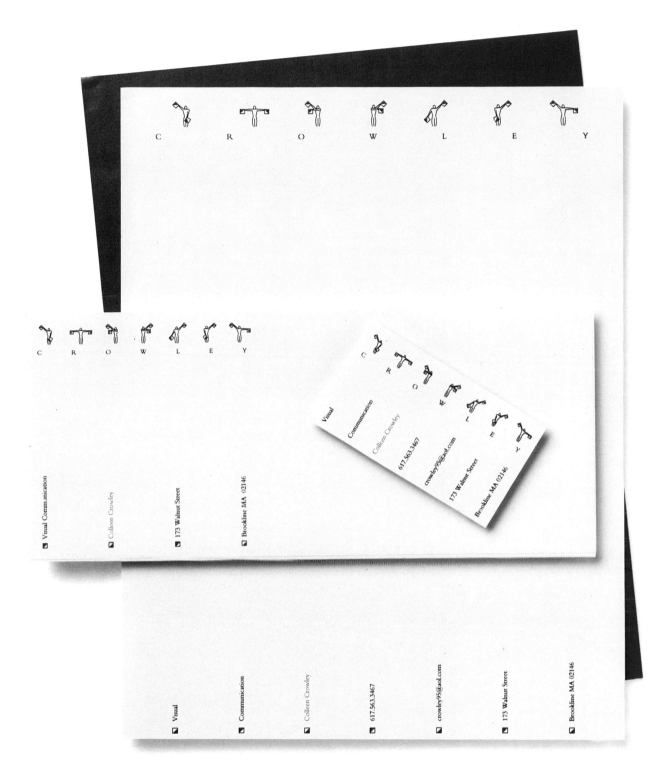

CLIENT: CROWLEY DESIGN
DESIGNER: COLLEEN CROWLEY
COUNTRY: USA
INDUSTRY: GRAPHIC DESIGN

1. **What is Trudy Cole-Zielanski?**
   ☐ a graphic designer
   ☐ an educator
   ☐ all of the above
   ☐ none of the above

2. **Where is TCZ?**
   ☐ Rt1 Box 362
     Mount Solon, VA 22843
   ☐ M114 Duke Hall
     James Madison University
     Harrisonburg, VA 22807
   ☐ all of the above
   ☐ none of the above

3. **How can she be reached?**
   ☐ by phone at 703-568-3488
   ☐ by phone at 703-350-2011
   ☐ by e-mail at
     IN%"FAC_TCOLEZIE
     @VAX2.ACS.JMU.EDU"
   ☐ all of the above
   ☐ none of the above

Trudy Cole-Zielanski
Rte 1 Box 362 Mount Solon VA 22843

s, Logos been published in national and international
rochures graphic design annuals. troubleshooter; prob-
illustra- lem solver; illustrator, etc. [Collog.]
trations, **Trú'dy Çöle-Zië'lan·ṣkĭ** n. Pol. pers. f. 1. (a)
posters, a graphic designer, as in *Trudy Cole-Zielanski*
rs, con- Design (b) an educator; associate prof. of graph-
oncepts, ic design 2. resident of Rte 1 box 362 Mount
aposition Solon, VA 22843-9607, phone 703-568-3488 3.
ements, inhabitant of Duke Hall M114, The School of
rs cata- Media Arts & Design, James Madison
gues University, Harrisonburg, VA 22807, phone
rs,mail- 703-350-2011 or 703-568-6216 4. E-mailer at
terheads IN%" FAC_TCOLEZIE@VAX2.ACS.JMU.EDU"
all cards faithful; loyal; constant; reliable; certain; as a

Score: _____

CLIENT: TRUDY COLE-ZIELANSKI DESIGN

DESIGN FIRM: TRUDY COLE-ZIELANSKI DESIGN

ART DIRECTOR/DESIGNER/ILLUSTRATOR: TRUDY COLE-ZIELANSKI

COUNTRY: USA

INDUSTRY: GRAPHIC DESIGN

SAGMEISTER INC.

NEW YORK

SAGMEISTER INC.

222 WEST 14th STREET

SUITE 15A

NEW YORK NY 10011

US of A

STYLE=FART

SAGMEISTER INC.

222 WEST 14th STREET NEW YORK NY 10011 US of A TEL (212) 647 1789 FAX (212) 647 1788

CLIENT: SAGMEISTER INC.

DESIGN FIRM: SAGMEISTER INC.

ART DIRECTOR/DESIGNER: STEFAN SAGMEISTER

COUNTRY: USA

INDUSTRY: GRAPHIC DESIGN

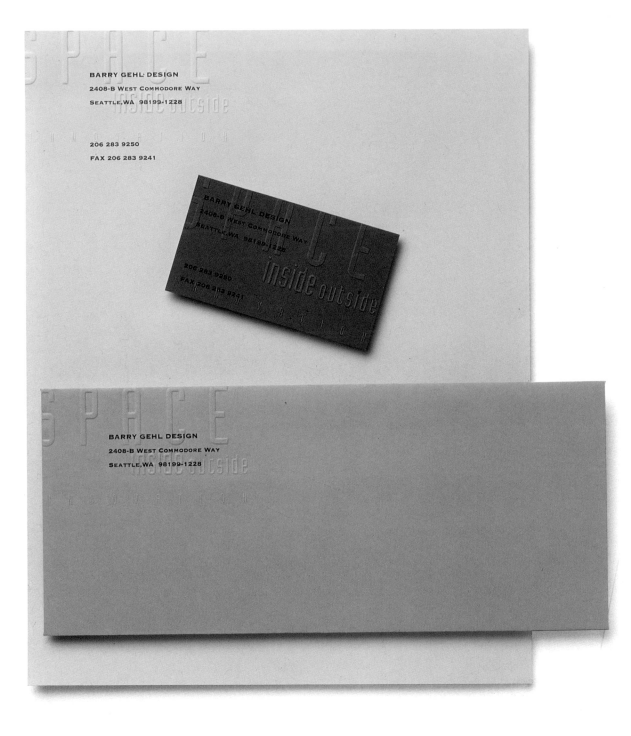

CLIENT: BARRY GEHL DESIGN

DESIGN FIRM: GEHL DESIGN

ART DIRECTOR/DESIGNER: JOYCE GEHL

COUNTRY: USA

INDUSTRY: INDUSTRIAL DESIGN/INDUSTRIE-DESIGN/DESIGN INDUSTRIEL

CLIENT/DESIGN FIRM: FACTOR DESIGN
ART DIRECTOR/ILLUSTRATOR: RÜDIGER GÖTZ
DESIGNERS: RÜDIGER GÖTZ, OLAF STEIN
COUNTRY: GERMANY
INDUSTRY: GRAPHIC DESIGN

CLIENT/DESIGN FIRM: PLUS DESIGN INC.
ART DIRECTORS: ANITA MEYER, KARIN FICKETT
DESIGNERS: ANITA MEYER, KARIN FICKETT, DINA ZACCAGNINI, MATTHEW MONK,
NICOLE JUEN, CAROLINA SENIOR, VERONICA MAJLONA
COUNTRY: USA
INDUSTRY: GRAPHIC DESIGN

CLIENT: NVIDIA CORPORATION
DESIGN FIRM: TOLLESON DESIGN
ART DIRECTORS: STEVEN TOLLESON, JENNIFER STERLING
DESIGNERS: STEVEN TOLLESON, JENNIFER STERLING, SUZANNE FRICKE
COUNTRY: USA
INDUSTRY: GRAPHIC DESIGN

CLIENT/DESIGN FIRM: THOMAS WELTNER
ART DIRECTOR/DESIGNER: THOMAS WELTNER
COUNTRY: GERMANY
INDUSTRY: GRAPHIC DESIGN

CLIENT: TROY M. LITTEN

ART DIRECTOR/DESIGNER: TROY M. LITTEN

COUNTRY: USA

INDUSTRY: DESIGNER

CLIENT: RIVERBEAR RETRIEVERS

DESIGN FIRM: EXECUTIVE ARTS INC.

ART DIRECTOR: RICHARD ANWYL

DESIGNER: MATT ROLLINS

ILLUSTRATOR: BILL MAYER

COUNTRY: USA

INDUSTRY: DOG TRAINERS AND KENNEL/HUNDEZUCHT UND -DRESSUR/

DRESSAGE ET ÉLEVAGE DE CHIENS

CLIENT: UNIVERSITY OF WASHINGTON SCHOOL OF MEDICINE
DESIGN FIRM: THE LEONHARDT GROUP
DESIGNERS: SUSAN CUMMINGS, TIM YOUNG
ILLUSTRATORS: TIM YOUNG, TRACI DABERKO
COUNTRY: USA
INDUSTRY: EDUCATION/AUSBILDUNG/FORMATION

CLIENT: DESIGN MILWAUKEE

DESIGN FIRM: BECKER DESIGN

ART DIRECTOR/DESIGNER: NEIL BECKER

COUNTRY: USA

INDUSTRY: GRAPHIC DESIGN/DESIGN GRAPHIQUE

CONFERENCE CENTER

340 NORTH
ESCONDIDO
BLVD

340 NORTH
ESCONDIDO
BLVD

ESCONDIDO
CALIFORNIA
92025

340 NORTH
ESCONDIDO
BLVD

CALIFORNIA CENTER FOR THE ARTS MUSEUM

340 NORTH
ESCONDIDO BLVD

ESCONDIDO
CALIFORNIA
92025

PH 619 738 4138
FX 619 739 0205

CLIENT: CALIFORNIA CENTER FOR THE ARTS
DESIGN FIRM: MIRES DESIGN, INC.
ART DIRECTOR/DESIGNER: JOHN BALL
COUNTRY: USA
INDUSTRY: VISUAL AND PERFORMING ARTS CENTER/
INSTITUT FÜR VISUELLE UND DARSTELLENDE KÜNSTE/
CENTRE D'ARTS VISUELS ET D'ARTS DE REPRÉSENTATION

CLIENT: A MINHA ESCOLA
DESIGN FIRM: ANTERO FERREIRA DESIGN
ART DIRECTOR: ANTERO FERREIRA
DESIGNER/ILLUSTRATOR: EDUARDO SOTTO MAYOR
COUNTRY: PORTUGAL
INDUSTRY: CHILDREN'S SCHOOL/GRUNDSCHULE/ECOLE PRIMAIRE

CLIENT: BURTON SNOWBOARDS

DESIGN FIRM: PAUL KAZA ASSOCIATES

ART DIRECTOR/DESIGNER: PAUL KAZA

COUNTRY: USA

INDUSTRY: SNOWBOARDING CHAMPIONSHIP/SNOWBOARD MEISTERSCHAFT/

CHAMPIONNAT DE SNOWBOARD

FESTIVAL COMMITTEE

Nestor Almendros (1930-92)

Michael Barker

Alan Bergman

Marilyn Bergman

Peter Biskind

Cynthia Brown

Fabiano Canosa

Elaine Charnov

Christine Choy

Jill Clayburgh

Jonathan Demme

Mark Diamond

Milos Forman

Costa Gavras

Geoffrey Gilmore

Henry Hampton

Marina Kaufman

Wendy Keys

Sidney Lumet

Bill Miles

Mira Nair

Marcel Ophuls

Alan Pakula

Hannah Pakula

Jacques Perrin

David Rabe

Edwin Rekosh

Ellen Schneider

Ousmane Sembene

Ron Silver

Tom Stoddard

Dan Talbot

Rachel Weintraub

Fred Wiseman

· · · · ·

Hamilton Fish, *Festival Director*

Bruni Burres, *Programmer*

Heather Harding, *Coordinator*

HUMAN RIGHTS WATCH

Robert L. Bernstein, *Chair.*

Kenneth Roth, *Executive Director*

485 Fifth Avenue

New York, NY 10017

Tel: 212 972-8400

Fax: 212 972-0905

HUMAN
RIGHTS
WATCH
INTERNATIONAL
FILM
FESTIVAL
1994

HUMAN RIGHTS WATCH INTERNATIONAL FILM FESTIVAL

CLIENT: HUMAN RIGHTS WATCH

ART DIRECTOR/DESIGNER: MARGARET MARCY

COUNTRY: USA

INDUSTRY: INTERNATIONAL HUMAN RIGHTS MONITORING/INTERNATIOANALE MENSCHENRECHTSORGANISATION/

ORGANISATION INTERNATIONALE DES DROITS DE L'HOMME

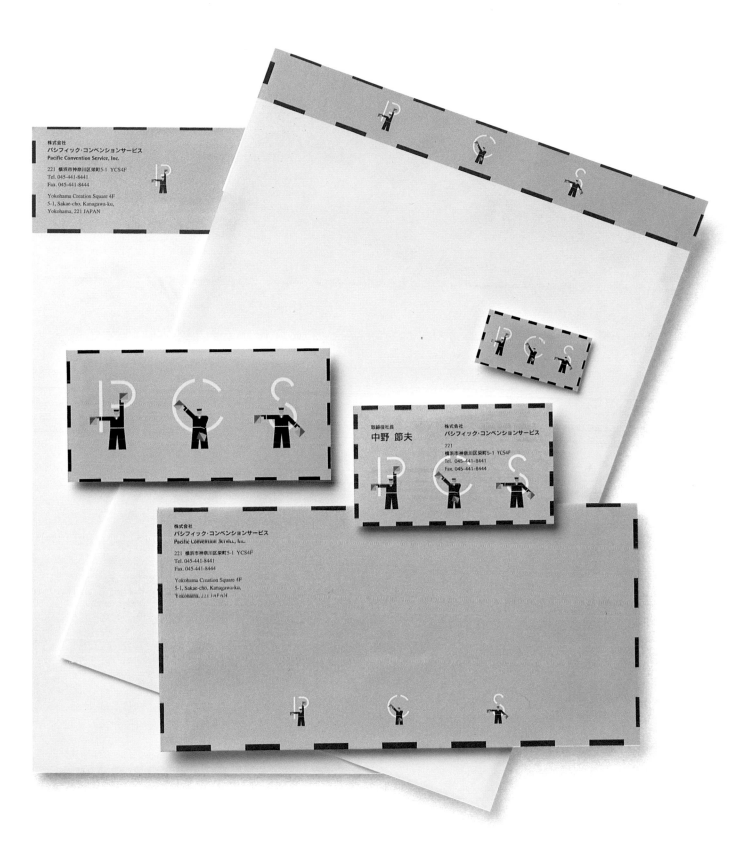

CLIENT: PACIFIC CONVENTION SERVICE, INC.

DESIGN FIRM: NDC GRAPHICS INC.

ART DIRECTOR: KENZO NAKAGAWA

DESIGNERS: KENZO NAKAGAWA, HIROYASU NOBUYAMA, SATOSHI MORIKAMI, HIROYUKI INDA

COUNTRY: JAPAN

INDUSTRY: CONVENTION SERVICE/ORGANISATION VON TAGUNGEN/

ORGANISATION DE CONGRÈS

CLIENT: TIMBER HILL FARM
DESIGN FIRM: JAGER DI PAOLO KEMP
CREATIVE DIRECTOR: MICHAEL JAGER
ART DIRECTOR: JANET JOHNSON
DESIGNER: CHRISTOPHER VICE
COUNTRY: USA
INDUSTRY: TIMBER FARM/NUTZWALD/EXPLOITATION FORESTIÈRE

☞ **Office**

5 Concourse Parkway

Suite 3100

Atlanta, Georgia

30328

☞ **Office**

5 Concourse Parkway

Suite 3100

Atlanta, Georgia

30328

☎ (404) 804-5830

🌿 **Farm**

Route 6

Moultrie, Georgia

31768

☎ (912) 985-1444

Ralph T. Clark

☞ **Office**
5 Concourse Parkway
Suite 3100
Atlanta, Georgia 30328

☎ (404) 804-5830

🌿 **Farm**
Route 6
Moultrie, Georgia 31760

☎ (912) 985-1444

C L I E N T : C L A R K B R O T H E R S F A R M S

D E S I G N F I R M : C O K E R G O L L E Y L T D .

A R T D I R E C T O R S : J A N E C O K E R , F R A N K G O L L E Y

D E S I G N E R / I L L U S T R A T O R : J U L I A M A H O O D

C O U N T R Y : U S A

I N D U S T R Y : P R O D U C E F A R M / L A N D W I R T S C H A F T / A G R I C U L T U R E

Lord Howe Island Board
—✳—
First floor, Phoenix House
1 Moncur Street, Woollahra
New South Wales
Australia 2025
Telephone 02 · 328 6999
Facsimile 02 · 363 5753

(THIS PAGE) CLIENT: LORD HOWE ISLAND BOARD DESIGN FIRM: HARCUS DESIGN ART DIRECTOR: ANNETTE HARCUS DESIGNER: ANNETTE HARCUS ILLUSTRATORS: ANNETTE HARCUS, MELINDA DUDLEY COUNTRY: AUSTRALIA INDUSTRY: GROWERS & EXPORTERS OF PALMS/PALMENANBAU & EXPORT/PALMERAIE & EXPORT ■ (OPPOSITE PAGE) CLIENT: PATRICIA FIELD DESIGNER: ESTER ARATEN COUNTRY: USA INDUSTRY: CLOTHING STORE/MODEBOUTIQUE/BOUTIQUE DE MODE patricia field 10 east 8th street new york, n.y 10003

patricia

FIELD

10 east 8th street new york, n.y 10003
tel 212 - 254 1699 fax 212 - 529 0834

patricia

FIELD

10 east 8th street new york, n.y 10003 tel 212 - 254 1699 fax 212 - 529 0834

patricia

FIELD

CLIENT: RIPPELSTEINS MEN'S FASHIONS
DESIGN FIRM: VAUGHN WEDEEN CREATIVE
ART DIRECTOR/DESIGNER/ILLUSTRATOR: RICK VAUGHN
COUNTRY: USA
INDUSTRY: MEN'S FASHION/MÄNNERMODE/CONFECTION POUR HOMMES

CLIENT: SCRAM
DESIGN FIRM: BRD DESIGN
ART DIRECTOR/DESIGNER: PETER KING ROBBINS
COUNTRY: USA
INDUSTRY: CLOTHING COMPANY/TEXTILFIRMA/FABRICANT DE VÊTEMENTS

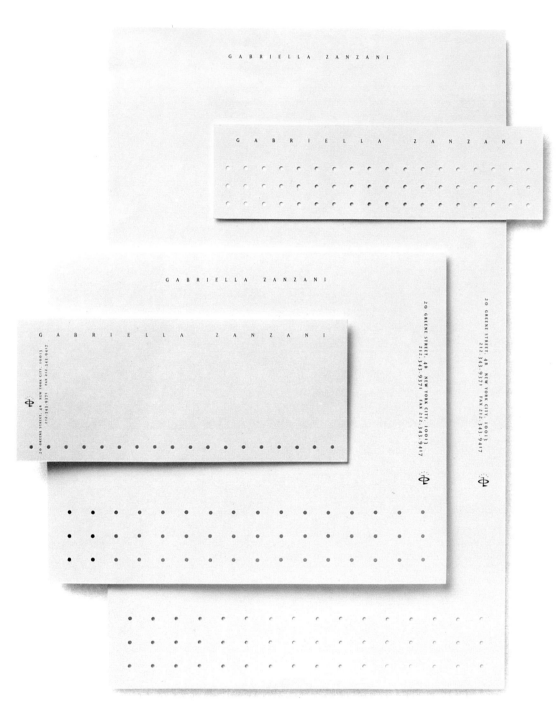

CLIENT: GABRIELLA ZANZANI
DESIGN FIRM: SPACE CRAFT
DESIGNER: SEBASTIAN KAUPERT
COUNTRY: USA
INDUSTRY: FASHION DESIGNER/MODE-DESIGNERIN/MODÉLISTE

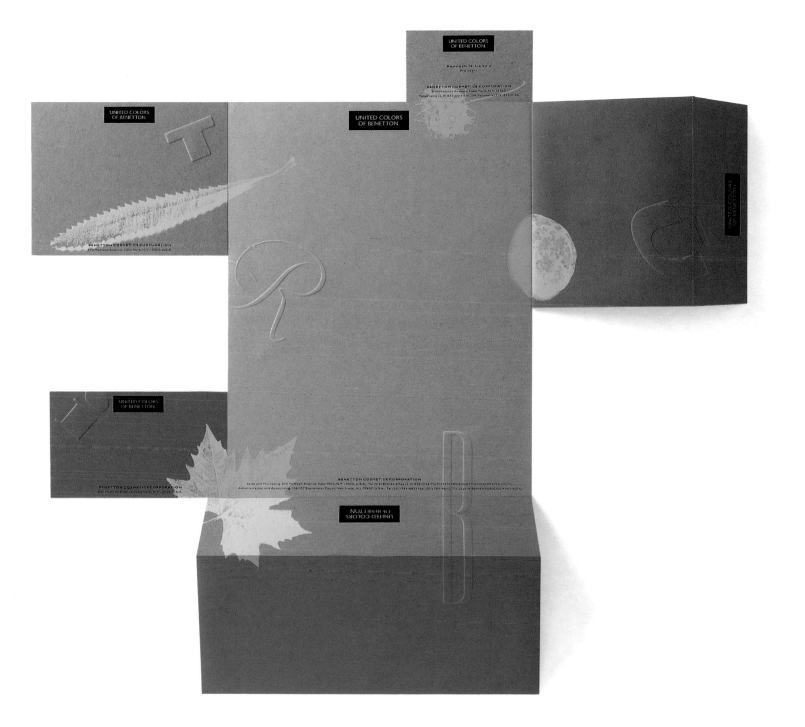

CLIENT: BENETTON

DESIGN FIRM: TAMOTSU YAGI DESIGN

ART DIRECTOR/DESIGNER: TAMOTSU YAGI

PHOTOGRAPHER: SHARON RISEDORPH

COUNTRY: USA

INDUSTRY: CLOTHING COMPANY/TEXTILFIRMA/FABRICANT DE VÊTEMENTS

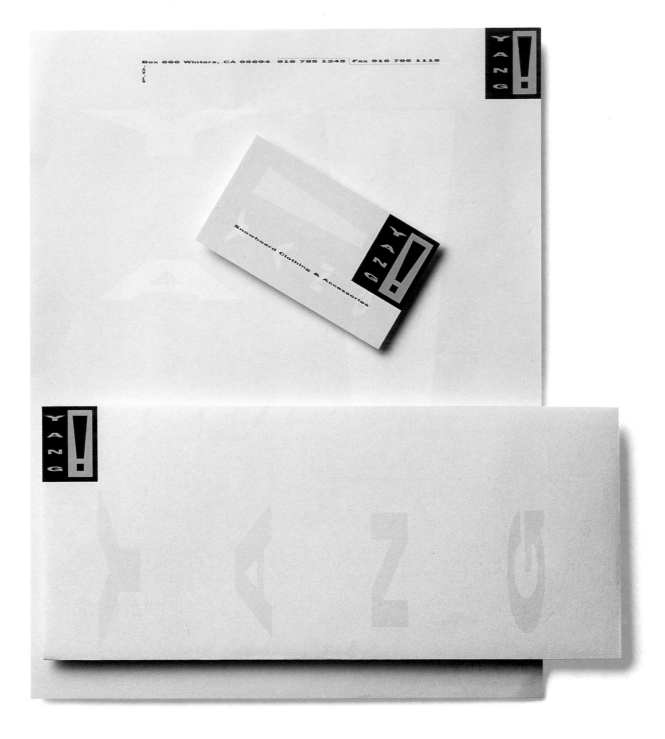

(THIS PAGE) CLIENT: YANG SNOWBOARDING DESIGN FIRM: TSANG, PROPP & GUERIN ART DIRECTOR: PAUL TSANG
DESIGNER: PAUL TSANG COUNTRY: USA INDUSTRY: SNOWBOARD CLOTHING/SNOWBOARD-MODE/MODE SNOWBOARD ■
(OPPOSITE PAGE) CLIENT: GABRIELE SKACH ART DIRECTOR: ALEXANDER SPANG DESIGNER: ALEXANDER SPANG
PHOTOGRAPHER: MICHAEL RATHMAYER COUNTRY: AUSTRIA INDUSTRY: FASHION DESIGNER/MODE-DESIGNERIN/MODÉLISTE

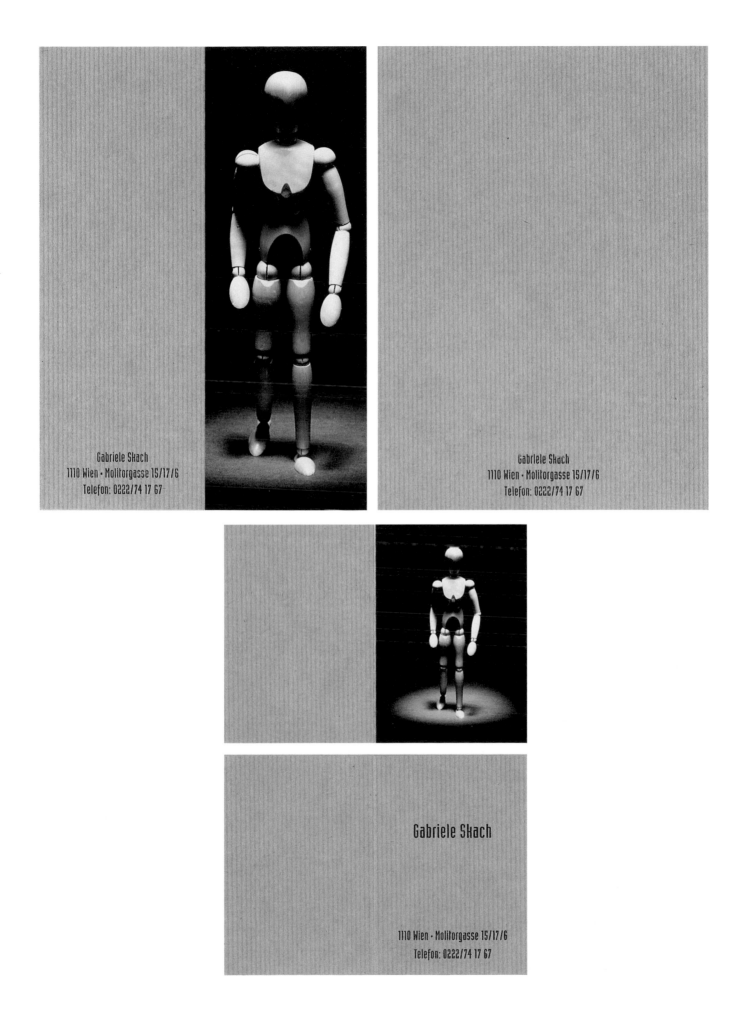

Gabriele Skach
1110 Wien · Molitorgasse 15/17/6
Telefon: 0222/74 17 67

Gabriele Skach
1110 Wien · Molitorgasse 15/17/6
Telefon: 0222/74 17 67

Gabriele Skach

1110 Wien · Molitorgasse 15/17/6
Telefon: 0222/74 17 67

CLIENT: BARTLETT WINERY

ART DIRECTOR/DESIGNER: LOUISE FILI

COUNTRY: USA

INDUSTRY: WINERY/WEINGUT/ETABLISSEMENT VINICOLE

CLIENT: L'AUBERGINE
DESIGN FIRM: CFD DESIGN
ART DIRECTOR: GREG FISHER
DESIGNERS: GREG FISHER, TRAVIS BUCKNER, STEVE DITKO
COUNTRY: USA
INDUSTRY: CATERING SERVICE/HAUSLIEFERDIENST VON LEBENSMITTELN/TRAITEUR

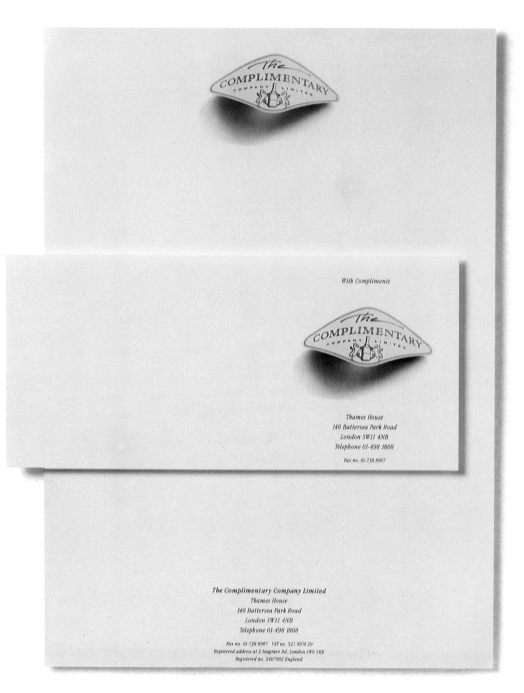

CLIENT: IDV
DESIGN FIRM: TUTSSELS
ART DIRECTOR: GLENN TUTSSEL
DESIGNER/ILLUSTRATOR: NICK HANSON
COUNTRY: GREAT BRITAIN
INDUSTRY: DISTILLERS AND VINTNERS/
DESTILLATEUR UND WEINHÄNDLER/
DISTILLATEUR ET NÉGOCIANT EN VINS

CHIP FISHER   PRESIDENT

27 EAST 92 STREET • NEW YORK, NY 10128 • (212) 831 5555

27 EAST 92 STREET • NEW YORK, NY 10128 • (212) 831 5555

(OPPOSITE) CLIENT: MR. CHIPS ICE CREAM STORE DESIGN FIRM: THE PUSHPIN GROUP ART DIRECTOR/DESIGNER: SEYMOUR CHWAST COUNTRY: USA INDUSTRY: ICE CREAM STORE/EISDIELE/MARCHAND DE GLACES ■ (THIS PAGE) CLIENT: ZIO RICCO DESIGN FIRM: THE LEONHARDT GROUP DESIGNERS: JANET KRUSE, TRACI DABERKO ILLUSTRATOR: JULIE PASCHKIS COUNTRY: USA INDUSTRY: COFFEE HOUSE/CAFÉ

SWEETISH HILL BAKERY 1120 WEST 6TH ST. AUSTIN, TX 78703 FAX.472.6041 512.472.7370

SWEETISH HILL BAKERY 1120 WEST 6TH ST. AUSTIN, TX 78703

BETH WIEDERAENDERS
PRODUCTION MANAGER

SWEETISH HILL BAKERY
1120 WEST 6TH ST.
AUSTIN, TEXAS 78703
FAX.472.6041
512.472.7370

CLIENT: SWEETISH HILL BAKERY

DESIGN FIRM: HIXO, INC.

ART DIRECTOR: TOM POTH

DESIGNERS: TOM POTH, MIKE HICKS

COUNTRY: USA

INDUSTRY: BAKERY/BÄCKEREI/BOULANGERIE

CLIENT: ANNE SEMMES

DESIGN FIRM: TONI SCHOWALTER DESIGN

ART DIRECTOR/DESIGNER: TONI SCHOWALTER

COUNTRY: USA

INDUSTRY: FOOD WRITER AND CONSULTANT/GASTROREPORTERIN UND -BERATERIN/

JOURNALISTE ET CONSEILLÈRE EN GASTRONOMIE

(OPPOSITE) CLIENT: BOSTON CHOCOLATE CO. DESIGN FIRM: WERNER DESIGN WERKS INC. DESIGNER/ILLUSTRATOR: SHARON WERNER
COUNTRY: USA INDUSTRY: CONFECTIONS/KONFISERIE/CONFISÉRIE ■ (ABOVE) CLIENT: HARVEST MARKET DESIGN FIRM: JAGER DI
PAOLA KEMP CREATIVE/ART DIRECTOR: MICHAEL JAGER DESIGNERS: MICHAEL JAGER, CALLIE JOHNSON, VICKI MCCAFFERTY
ILLUSTRATOR: DAN KROVATIN COUNTRY: USA INDUSTRY: FOOD MARKET/LEBENSMITTELMARKT/MARCHÉ FRUITS ET LÉGUMES

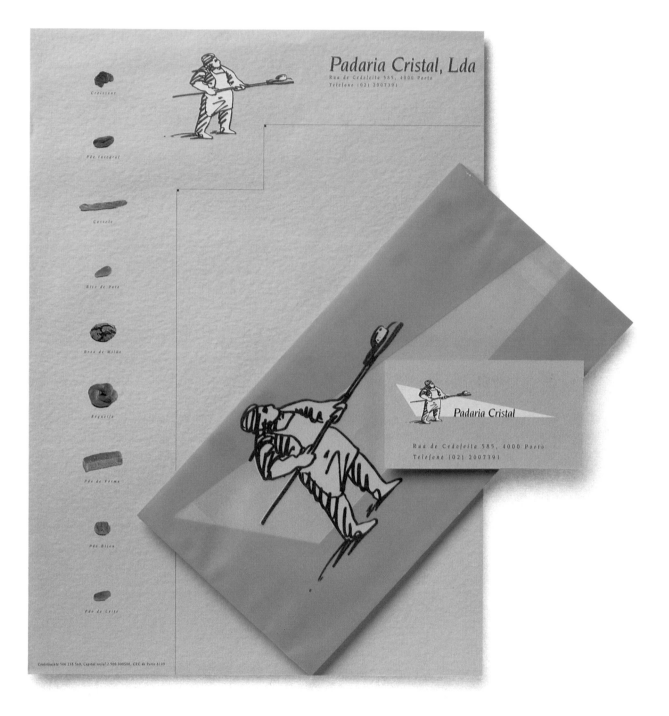

CLIENT: PADARIA CRISTAL

DESIGN FIRM: ANTERO FERREIRA DESIGN

ART DIRECTOR: ANTERO FERREIRA

DESIGNER: EDUARDO SOTTO MAYOR

ILLUSTRATORS: OSCAR DE ALMEIDA, EDUARDO SOTTO MAYOR

COUNTRY: PORTUGAL

INDUSTRY: BAKERY/BÄCKEREI/BOULANGERIE

CLIENT: BONE DRY BEER
DESIGNER: MARGO CHASE DESIGN
PRINTER: BURDGE, INC.
COUNTRY: USA
INDUSTRY: BREWERY/BRAUEREI/BRASSERIE

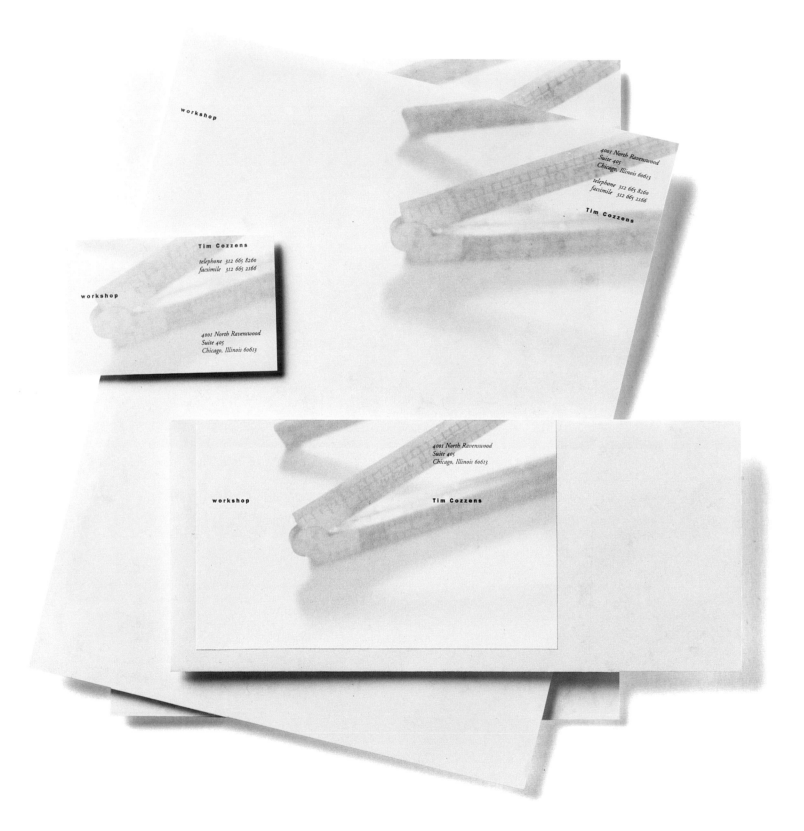

(ABOVE) Client: WORKSHOP TIM COZZENS Design Firm: MUELLER BAKER ASSOC. Art Director: KRISTI MUELLER Designers: KRISTI MUELLER, CLINTON MEYER Country: USA Industry: FURNITURE DESIGNER AND MANUFACTURER/MÖBELENTWURF UND -HERSTELLUNG/DESIGNER ET FABRICANT DE MEUBLES ■ (OPPOSITE PAGE) Client: WIELAND FURNITURE CO. Design Firm: DUFFY DESIGN Art Director/Designer: NEIL POWELL Country: USA Industry: FURNITURE COMPANY/MÖBELHERSTELLER/FABRICANT DE MEUBLES

CLIENT: ANTON KRÄUTLER

DESIGN FIRM: KÖHNLEIN GRAFIK DESIGN

ART DIRECTOR/ILLUSTRATOR: FRITZ TILL KÖHNLEIN

COUNTRY: AUSTRIA

INDUSTRY: FURNITURE RESTORATION/MÖBELRESTAURATIONEN/

RESTAURATION DE MEUBLES

Client: HOLZWERKSTATT
Art Director: CLAUDIA BRUST-SCHWING
Country: GERMANY
Industry: CARPENTRY & INTERIOR DESIGN/SCHREINEREI & INNENARCHITEKTUR/
MENUISERIE & DÉCORATION D'INTÉRIEURS

CLIENTS: SAUNDERS HOTELS, COPLEY SQUARE HOTELS
DESIGN FIRM: MIDNIGHT OIL STUDIOS
ART DIRECTOR/DESIGNER/ILLUSTRATOR: KATHRYN KLEIN
COUNTRY: USA
INDUSTRY: HOTELS

CLIENT: THE STONE KITCHEN
DESIGN FIRM: GEER DESIGN, INC.
ART DIRECTOR/DESIGNER/ILLUSTRATOR: MARK GEER
PHOTOGRAPHER: KEY SANDERS
COUNTRY: USA
INDUSTRY: CATERING COMPANY/ESSEN AUF RÄDERN/SOCIÉTÉ DE RESTAURATION

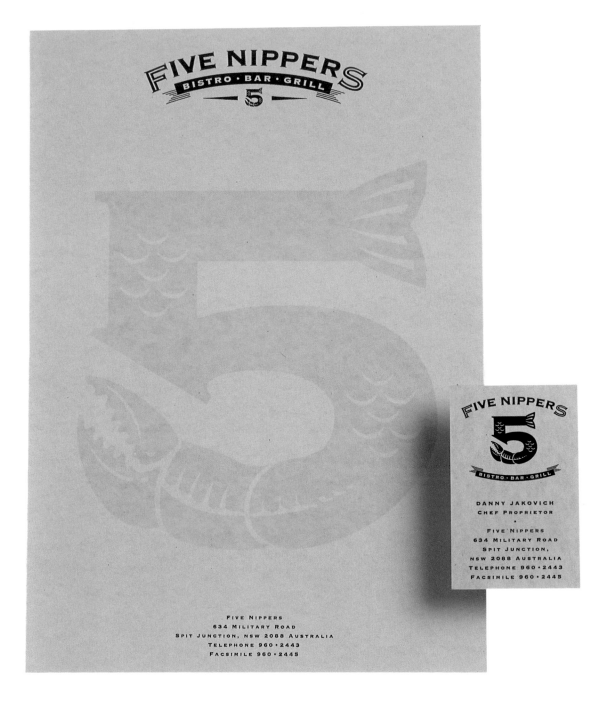

CLIENT: FIVE NIPPERS

DESIGN FIRM: MARIO MILOSTIC DESIGN

DESIGNER: MARIO MILOSTIC

COUNTRY: AUSTRALIA

INDUSTRY: BAR/RESTAURANT

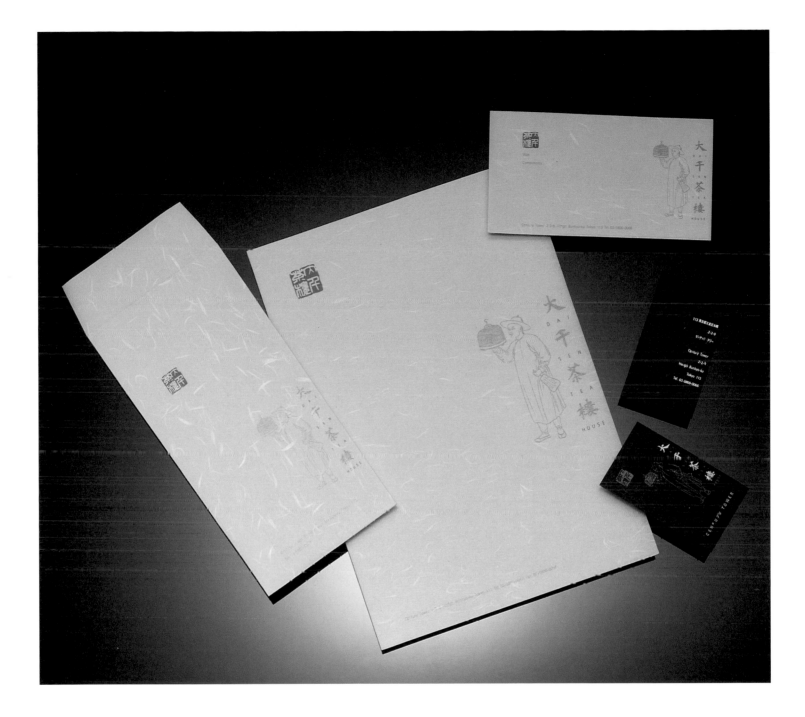

CLIENT: DAI SEN TEA HOUSE

DESIGN FIRM: ALAN CHAN DESIGN COMPANY

ART DIRECTOR: ALAN CHAN

COUNTRY: HONG KONG

INDUSTRY: TEA HOUSE/TEEHAUS/SALON DE THÉ

CLIENT: LIVERPOOL RESTAURANT & PUB
DESIGN FIRM: FREE RANGE DESIGN
DESIGNER: DAVID HUGHES
COUNTRY: USA
INDUSTRY: RESTAURANT

CLIENT: CAPONS ROTISSERIE CHICKEN RESTAURANT

DESIGN FIRM: HORNALL ANDERSON DESIGN WORKS, INC.

ART DIRECTOR: JACK ANDERSON

DESIGNERS: JACK ANDERSON, DAVID BATES

ILLUSTRATORS: DAVID BATES, GEORGE TANAGI

COUNTRY: USA

INDUSTRY: ROTISSERIE CHICKEN RESTAURANT/HÄHNCHENGRILL/RÔTISSERIE

CLIENT: VAUCLUSE HOUSE TEAROOMS
DESIGN FIRM: HARCUS DESIGN
ART DIRECTOR/DESIGNER: ANNETTE HARCUS
ILLUSTRATOR: MELINDA DUDLEY
COUNTRY: AUSTRALIA
INDUSTRY: TEAROOM/TEESTUBEN/SALON DE THÉ

CLIENT: SAKAEGAWA JAPANESE RESTAURANT
DESIGN FIRM: CETRIC LEUNG DESIGN
ART DIRECTOR: CETRIC LEUNG
COUNTRY: HONG KONG
INDUSTRY: JAPANESE RESTAURANT/JAPANISCHES RESTAURANT/
RESTAURANT JAPONAIS

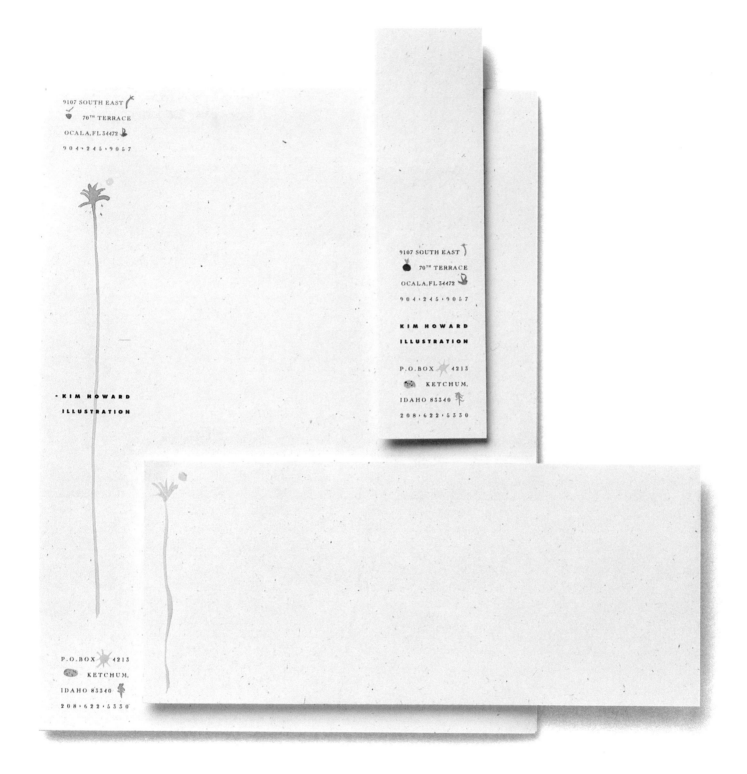

CLIENT: KIM HOWARD
DESIGN FIRM: SACKETT DESIGN ASSOCIATES
ART DIRECTOR: MARK SACKETT
DESIGNERS: MARK SACKETT, JAMES SAKAMOTO
ILLUSTRATOR: KIM HOWARD
COUNTRY: USA
INDUSTRY: ILLUSTRATOR/ILLUSTRATORIN/ILLUSTRATRICE

CLIENT: ELEANOR ADAM
ART DIRECTOR: HAMAR COHN
ILLUSTRATOR: ELEANOR ADAM
COUNTRY: USA
INDUSTRY: CHILDREN'S BOOK ILLUSTRATOR/KINDERBUCH-ILLUSTRATORIN/
ILLUSTRATRICE DE LIVRES D'ENFANTS

CLIENT: STEVEN LOGOLUSO

DESIGN FIRM: PH.D

ART DIRECTORS: CLIVE PIERCY, MICHAEL HODGSON

DESIGNER: MICHAEL HODGSON

ILLUSTRATOR: PAUL LANDACRE

COUNTRY: USA

INDUSTRY: LANDSCAPE ARCHITECTURE/LANDSCHAFTSARCHITEKTUR/

ARCHITECTES PAYSAGISTES

CLIENT: LANCE LICHTER

DESIGN FIRM: BECKER·DESIGN

ART DIRECTOR/DESIGNER: NEIL BECKER

COUNTRY: USA

INDUSTRY: ATTORNEY/ANWALT/AVOCAT

CLIENT: RUBIN GLICKMAN

ART DIRECTOR: PRIMO ANGELI

DESIGNER: PHILIPPE BECKER

PRODUCTION MANAGER: ERIC KUBLY

COUNTRY: USA

INDUSTRY: ATTORNEY/ANWALT/AVOCAT

CLIENT: WU HAN EVERTOP MACHINERY CO.
ART DIRECTOR/DESIGNER/ILLUSTRATOR: YONGZHI WANG
COUNTRY: CHINA
INDUSTRY: MACHINERY/MASCHINENBAU/
CONSTRUCTION DE MACHINES

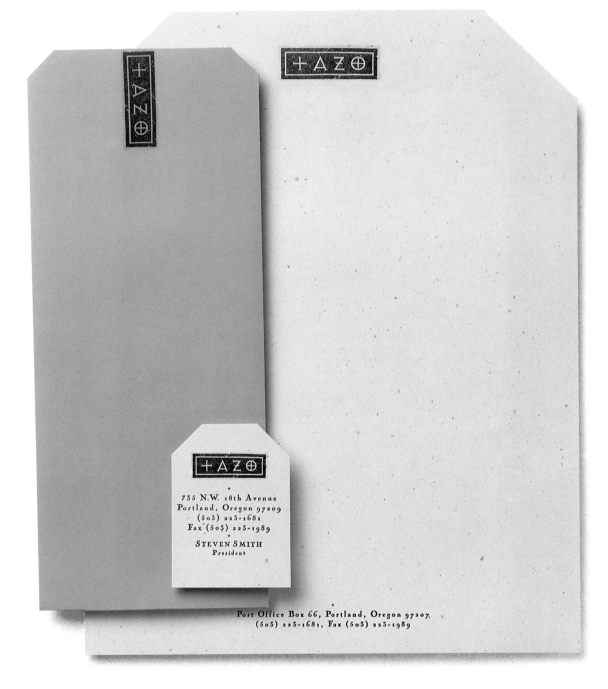

+AZ⊕

+AZ⊕

+AZ⊕
+
735 N.W. 18th Avenue
Portland, Oregon 97209
(503) 223-1681
Fax (503) 223-1989
+
STEVEN SMITH
President

+
Post Office Box 66, Portland, Oregon 97207,
(503) 223-1681, Fax (503) 223-1989

CLIENT: TAZO TEA

DESIGN FIRM: SANDSTROM DESIGN

ART DIRECTOR/DESIGNER: STEVEN SANDSTROM

COUNTRY: USA

INDUSTRY: TEA COMPANY/TEEHAUS

CLIENT: APACHE MOTORWORKS, INC.

DESIGN FIRM: NEXT WORLD DESIGN, INC.

ART DIRECTOR: KEN LAIVINS

DESIGNERS: GLEN LAIVINS, TIM CLEMENS

PHOTOGRAPHER: MARK STEEL

COUNTRY: USA

INDUSTRY: CUSTOM MOTORCYCLE MANUFACTURER/

SPEZIALANFERTIGUNG VON MOTORRÄDERN/

FABRICANT DE MOTOS SUR COMMANDE

GPF INC · 2360 NORTH STANLEY PLACE · MILWAUKEE WISCONSIN 53212

GPF INC · 2360 NORTH STANLEY PLACE · MILWAUKEE WISCONSIN 53212
TEL 414·265·8225 · FAX 414·265·8275 · 1·800·282·2360

Client: GPF
Design Firm: Barnes Design Office
Art Director/Designer: Jeff Barnes
Country: USA
Industry: Furniture Company/Möbelhersteller/Fabricant de Meubles

CLIENT: DELEO CLAY TILE
DESIGN FIRM: MIRES DESIGN, INC.
ART DIRECTOR/DESIGNER: JOSE SERRANO
ILLUSTRATOR: NANCY STAHL
COUNTRY: USA
INDUSTRY: CLAY TILE MANUFACTURER/
HERSTELLER VON KERAMIKFLIESEN/
FABRICANT DE CARREAUX EN CÉRAMIQUE

CLIENT: ACME RUBBER STAMP CO.

DESIGN FIRM: PETERSON & COMPANY

ART DIRECTOR/DESIGNER: DAVE ELIASON

COUNTRY: USA

INDUSTRY: RUBBER STAMP MANUFACTURER/

STEMPELHERSTELLER/

FABRICANT DE TIMBRES

Client: TOTO NEW CONCEPT GROUP

Design Firm: SAGMEISTER INC.

Art Director: STEFAN SAGMEISTER

Designers: STEFAN SAGMEISTER, VERONICA OH

Photographer: MICHAEL GRIMM

Country: USA

Industry: BATHROOM APPLIANCES/

SANITÄRE ANLAGEN/INSTALLATIONS SANITAIRES

CLIENT: DAVID HERNANDEZ

DESIGN FIRM: SULLIVANPERKINS

ART DIRECTOR/DESIGNER: ART GARCIA

COUNTRY: USA

INDUSTRY: AUTO MECHANIC/AUTOMECHANIKER/

MÉCANICIEN SUR AUTO

KFZ.-MEISTERBETRIEB · KENDZIA & RIEMENSCHNEIDER · 44143 DORTMUND-WAMBEL · LÜCKESTRASSE 29

KENDZIA & RIEMENSCHNEIDER

KENDZIA & RIEMENSCHNEIDER

KFZ.-MEISTERBETRIEB · 44143 DORTMUND-WAMBEL
LÜCKESTRASSE 29 · TELEFON: 0231-59 74 91

KENDZIA & RIEMENSCHNEIDER

KFZ.-MEISTERBETRIEB · 44143 DORTMUND-WAMBEL
LÜCKESTRASSE 29 · TELEFON: 0231-59 74 91

KFZ.-MEISTERBETRIEB · 44143 DORTMUND-WAMBEL
LÜCKESTRASSE 29 · TELEFON: 0231-59 74 91
BANKVERBINDUNG: POSTGIRO DORTMUND
KONTO-NUMMER: 3820 72 463 · BLZ 440 100 46

CLIENT: KENDZIA & RIEMENSCHNEIDER
DESIGN FIRM: REKLAME
DESIGNER: UWE GÖRLICH
COUNTRY: GERMANY
INDUSTRY: AUTO MECHANIC/KFZ-MEISTERBETRIEB/
MÉCANIQUE SUR AUTO

CLIENT: COWBOY ARTISTS OF AMERICA
DESIGN FIRM: AFTER HOURS
ART DIRECTOR: RUSS HAAN
DESIGNER: TODD FEDELL
PHOTOGRAPHER: BILL TIMMERMAN
COUNTRY: USA
INDUSTRY: ARTISTS ASSOCIATION/KÜNSTLERVEREINIGUNG/
ASSOCIATION D'ARTISTES

CLIENT: INDIANAPOLIS ART CENTER
DESIGN FIRM: YOUNG & LARAMORE
CREATIVE DIRECTOR/ILLUSTRATOR: DAVID YOUNG
ART DIRECTOR: CAROLYN HADLOCK
COUNTRY: USA
INDUSTRY: ART CENTER/KULTURZENTRUM/
CENTRE CULTUREL

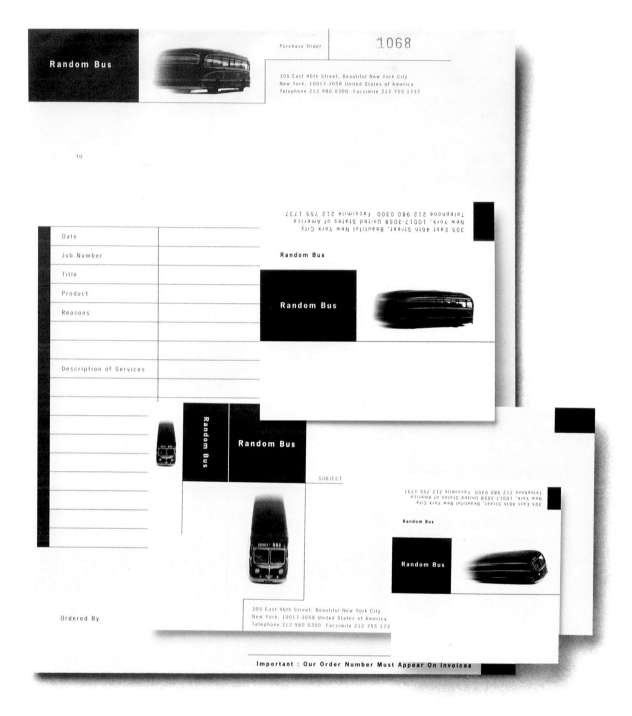

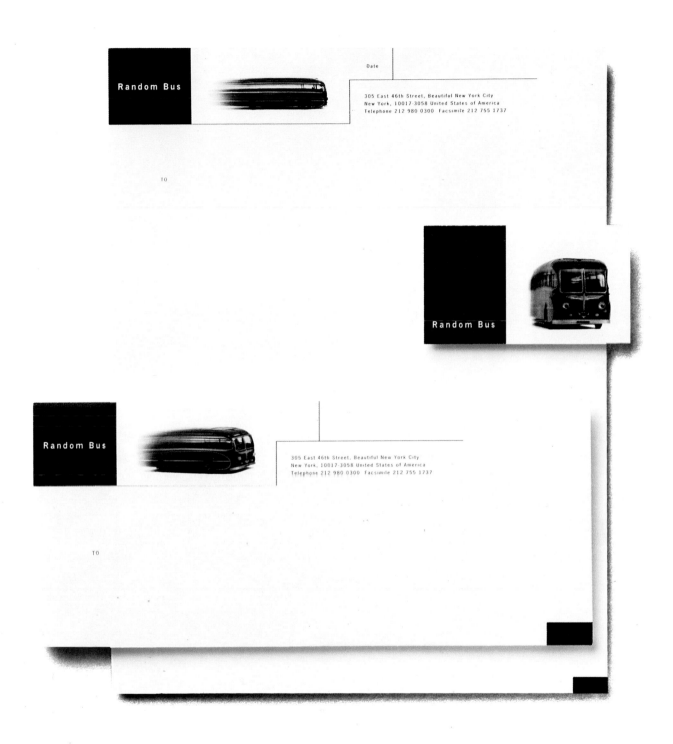

(THIS SPREAD)

CLIENT: RANDOM BUS

DESIGN FIRM: SAGMEISTER INC.

ART DIRECTOR: STEFAN SAGMEISTER

DESIGNER: ERIC ZIM

PHOTOGRAPHER: TOM SCHIERLITZ

COUNTRY: USA

INDUSTRY: MUSIC STUDIO/AUFNAHMESTUDIO/

STUDIO D'ENREGISTREMENT

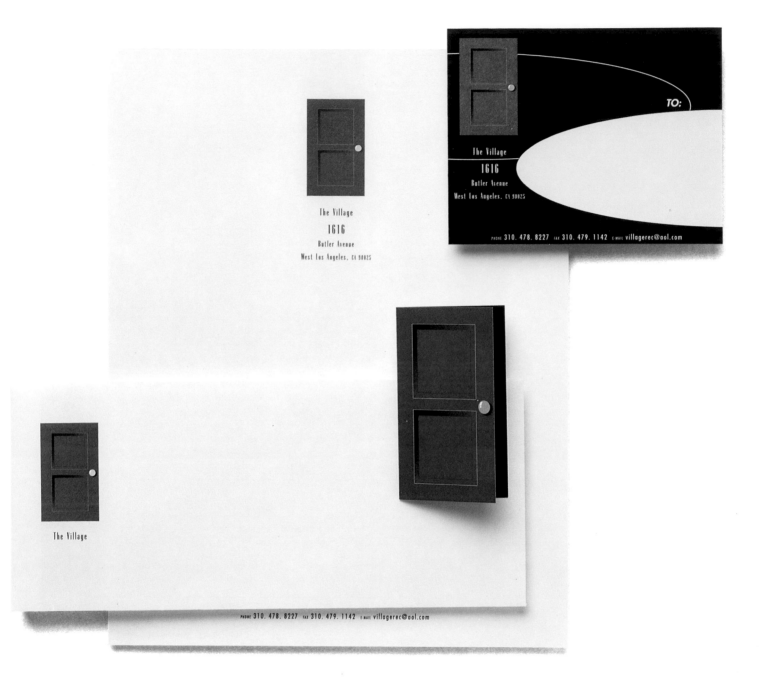

Client: THE VILLAGE
Design Firm: MIKE SALISBURY COMMUNICATIONS
Art Director: MIKE SALISBURY
Designers: MIKE SALISBURY, MARY EVELYN MCGOUGH
Illustrator: RAFAEL PEIXOTO FERREIRA
Country: USA
Industry: RECORDING STUDIO/AUFNAHMESTUDIO/
STUDIO D'ENREGISTREMENT

CLIENT: MC EUROPE

DESIGN FIRM: UFFINDELL & WEST

ART DIRECTOR/DESIGNER: DAVID O'HIGGINS

COUNTRY: GREAT BRITAIN

INDUSTRY: MUSIC SERVICE TARGETED AT CABLE OPERATORS/

MUSIKDIENST FÜR KABELBETREIBER/

SERVICE DE MUSIQUE CABLÉE

CLIENT: RECORD SERVICE

DESIGN FIRM: FELDER GRAFIK DESIGN

ART DIRECTOR/DESIGNER: PETER FELDER

ILLUSTRATOR: PETER FELDER

COUNTRY: AUSTRIA

INDUSTRY: RECORD DISTRIBUTION/MUSIKVERTRIEB/

SOCIÉTÉ DE DISTRIBUTION

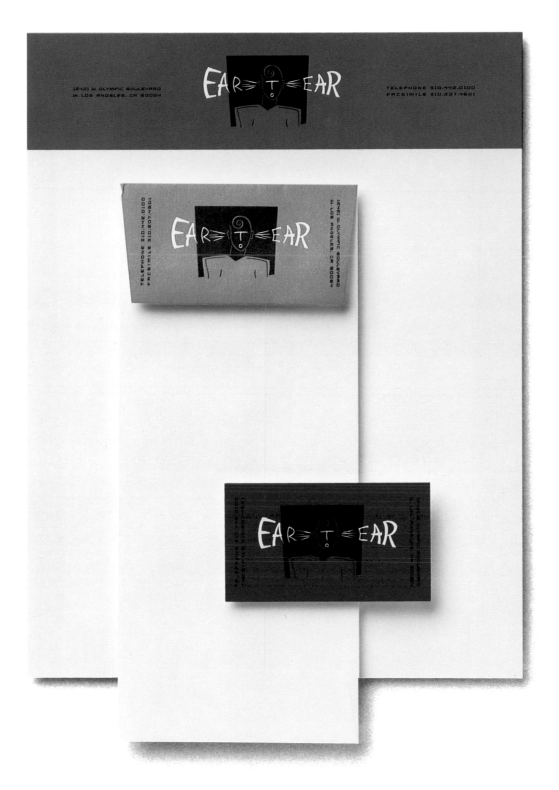

Client: EAR TO EAR
Design Firm: MIRES DESIGN, INC.
Art Director/Designer: SCOTT MIRES
Illustrator: TRACY SABIN
Country: USA
Industry: MUSIC PRODUCTION HOUSE/
MUSIKPRODUKTIONEN/SOCIÉTÉ DE PRODUCTION

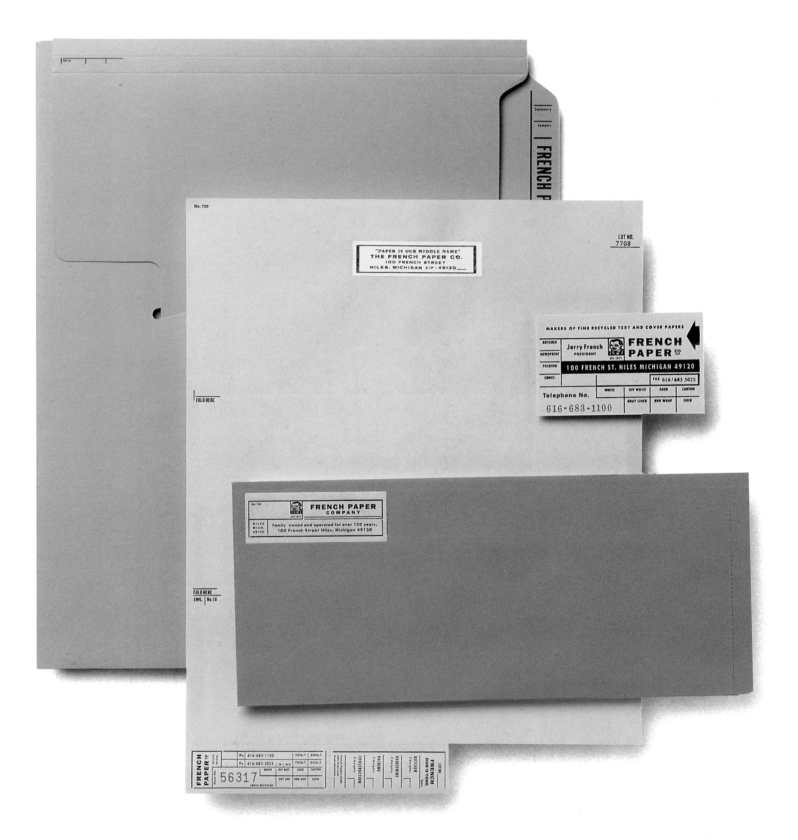

(OPPOSITE) CLIENT: FRENCH PAPER CO. DESIGN FIRM: CHARLES S. ANDERSON DESIGN COMPANY ART DIRECTOR: CHARLES S. ANDERSON DESIGNERS: CHARLES S. ANDERSON, TODD PIPER-HAUSWIRTH ILLUSTRATOR: CSA ARCHIVE COUNTRY: USA INDUSTRY: PAPER COMPANY/PAPIERHERSTELLER/FABRICANT DE PAPIER ■ (THIS PAGE) CLIENT: ROLAND SCHNEIDER DESIGN FIRM/ART DIRECTOR/ DESIGNER/ILLUSTRATOR: SCHNEIDER + PARTNER COUNTRY: GERMANY INDUSTRY: PHOTOGRAPHER/PHOTOGRAPH/PHOTOGRAPHE

CLIENT: MARK HOOPER PHOTOGRAPHY
DESIGN FIRM: SANDSTROM DESIGN
ART DIRECTOR/DESIGNER: STEVEN SANDSTROM
COUNTRY: USA
INDUSTRY: PHOTOGRAPHY/FOTOGRAFIE/PHOTOGRAPHIE

CLIENT: TOP PHOTOGRAPHY

DESIGN FIRM: MARIO GODBOUT DESIGN

ART DIRECTOR/DESIGNER: MARIO GODBOUT

PHOTOGRAPHER: TOP PHOTOGRAPHY

COUNTRY: CANADA

INDUSTRY: PHOTOGRAPHY/FOTOGRAFIE/PHOTOGRAPHIE

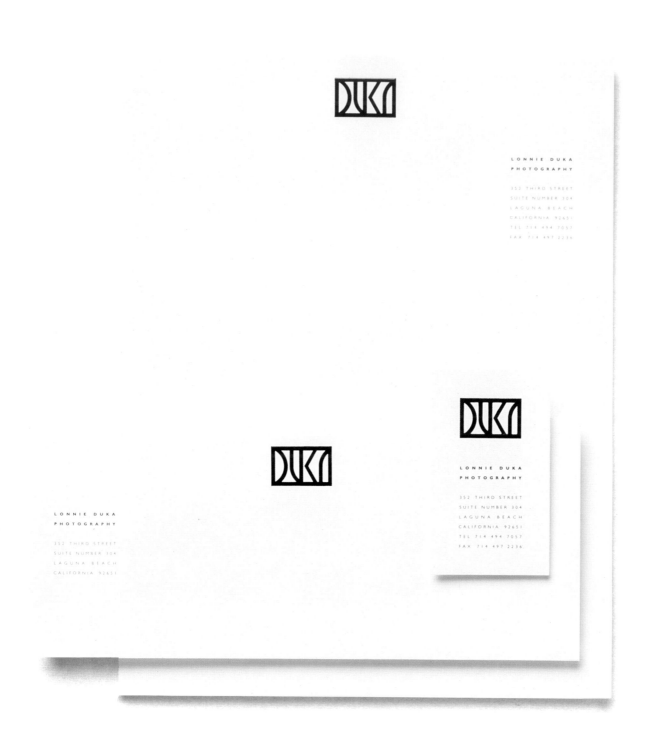

(THIS PAGE) Client: LONNIE DUKA PHOTOGRAPHY Design Firm: DULA GERRIE DESIGN Art Director/Designer: MICHAEL DULA Country: USA Industry: PHOTOGRAPHER/PHOTOGRAPH/PHOTOGRAPHE ■ (OPPOSITE PAGE) Client: ANDY KINGSBURY Design Firm: CHARLES S. ANDERSON DESIGN COMPANY Art Director: CHARLES S. ANDERSON Designer: JOEL TEMPLIN Country: USA Industry: PHOTOGRAPHY/FOTOGRAFIE/PHOTOGRAPHIE

Client: ROGER RICHTER
Designer: ESTHER LAUTH
Country: GERMANY
Industry: PHOTOGRAPHY/FOTOGRAFIE/PHOTOGRAPHIE

CLIENT: PAUL ELLEDGE

DESIGN FIRM: VSA PARTNERS, INC.

ART DIRECTOR: JAMES KOVAL

DESIGNERS: JAMES KOVAL, JENNIFFER WIESS

PHOTOGRAPHER: PAUL ELLEDGE

COUNTRY: USA

INDUSTRY: PHOTOGRAPHY/FOTOGRAFIE/PHOTOGRAPHIE

CLIENT: VANDERSCHUIT STUDIO INC.

DESIGN FIRM: MIRES DESIGN, INC.

ART DIRECTOR/DESIGNER: JOSE SERRANO

PHOTOGRAPHER: CARL VANDERSCHUIT

COUNTRY: USA

INDUSTRY: PHOTOGRAPHY/FOTOGRAFIE/PHOTOGRAPHIE

CLIENT: WALTERS PHOTOGRAPHIC
DESIGN FIRM: S.D. ZYNE
ART DIRECTOR/DESIGNER: SPENCER WALTERS
PHOTOGRAPHER: ELIZABETH WALTERS
COUNTRY: USA
INDUSTRY: PHOTOGRAPHY/FOTOGRAFIE/PHOTOGRAPHIE

CLIENT: PHOTOGRAPHIC PICTURES
DESIGN FIRM: LEO BURNETT DESIGN GROUP
ART DIRECTOR/DESIGNER: PATRICK DALY
COUNTRY: HONG KONG
INDUSTRY: PHOTOGRAPHY/FOTOGRAFIE/PHOTOGRAPHIE

CLIENT: KIRKI SCHULTZ

DESIGN FIRM: KILTER INCORPORATED

ART DIRECTOR/DESIGNER: DAVID RICHARDSON

COUNTRY: USA

INDUSTRY: PHOTOGRAPHY/FOTOGRAFIE/PHOTOGRAPHIE

CLIENT: STEVEN MCDONALD

DESIGN FIRM: PIVOT DESIGN, INC.

ART DIRECTOR: BROCK HALDEMAN

DESIGNERS: BROCK HALDEMAN, JIM LARMON

COUNTRY: USA

INDUSTRY: PHOTOGRAPHY/FOTOGRAFIE/PHOTOGRAPHIEPHE

CLIENT: DARRELL EAGER
DESIGN FIRM: CHARLES S. ANDERSON DESIGN COMPANY
ART DIRECTORS: CHARLES S. ANDERSON, TODD PIPER-HAUSWIRTH
DESIGNER: TODD PIPER-HAUSWIRTH
COUNTRY: USA
INDUSTRY: PHOTOGRAPHER/PHOTOGRAPH/PHOTOGRAPHE

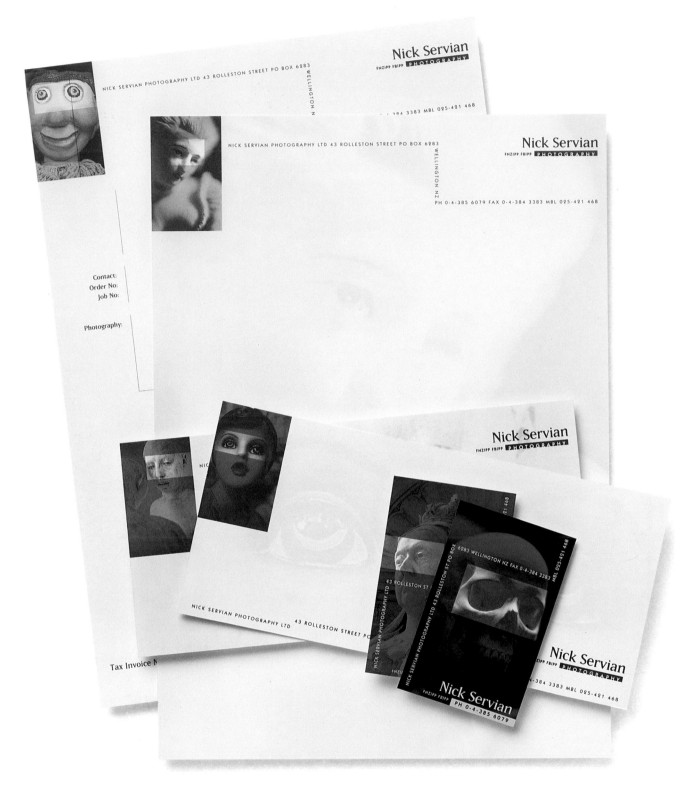

CLIENT: NICK SERVIAN

DESIGN FIRM: BNA DESIGN

ART DIRECTOR: GRENVILLE MAIN

DESIGNER: JASON O'HARA

PHOTOGRAPHER: NICK SERVIAN

COUNTRY: NEW ZEALAND

INDUSTRY: PHOTOGRAPHY/FOTOGRAFIE/PHOTOGRAPHIE

CLIENT: PAM PAULSON
DESIGN FIRM: MICHAEL OSBORNE DESIGN
ART DIRECTOR: MICHAEL OSBORNE
DESIGNER/ILLUSTRATOR: ANNA MISHINA
COUNTRY: USA
INDUSTRY: PRINTER/DRUCKEREI/IMPRIMERIE

(THIS PAGE) CLIENT: DRUCKEREI KOLL DESIGN FIRM: WOLFGANG HASLINGER GRAPHIK/DESIGN ART DIRECTOR/DESIGNER: WOLFGANG HASLINGER ILLUSTRATOR: WOLFGANG HASLINGER COUNTRY: AUSTRIA INDUSTRY: PRINTER/DRUCKEREI/IMPRIMERIE ■ (OPPOSITE PAGE) CLIENT: SIOUX PRINTING DESIGN FIRM: PARAGON DESIGN INTERNATIONAL INC. ART DIRECTOR: JOHN RACILA DESIGNER: BOB GAILEN PHOTOGRAPHER: TOM PETROFF COUNTRY: USA INDUSTRY: PRINTER/DRUCKEREI/IMPRIMERIE

Client: IMA-PRESS
Design Firm: KITAJEVA ART-DESIGN STUDIO
Art Director/Designer/Illustrator: JELENA KITAJEVA
Country: RUSSIA
Industry: PUBLISHING HOUSE AND GALLERY/VERLAG UND GALERIE/
MAISON D'ÉDITION ET GALERIE

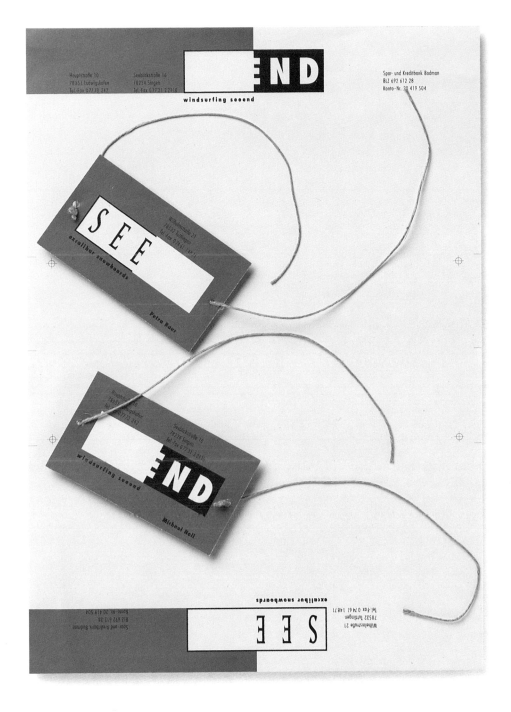

CLIENT: WINDSURFING SEEEND

DESIGN FIRM: D-WERK

DESIGNER: TOM MAIER

COUNTRY: GERMANY

INDUSTRY: WIND SURFING AND SNOWBOARD SHOPS/

WINDSURF- UND SNOWBOARD LÄDEN/

MAGASINS DE WINDSURF ET SNOWBOARDS

CLIENT: CANADIAN OUTBACK ADVENTURE COMPANY
DESIGN FIRM: ION DESIGN INC.
ART DIRECTOR: DAVID COATES
DESIGNER/ILLUSTRATOR: ROD ROODENBURG
COUNTRY: CANADA
INDUSTRY: ADVENTURE TRAVELING/ABENTEUERREISEN/VOYAGES D'AVENTURES

CLIENT: RANCHO ALEGRE

DESIGN FIRM: BAUCH DESIGN

ART DIRECTOR/DESIGNER: NANCY BAUCH

WRITER: JOHN PACKER

COUNTRY: USA

INDUSTRY: WESTERN GIFT STORE/

GESCHENKBOUTIQUE FÜR WESTERN-ARTIKEL/

MAGASIN D'ARTICLES 'WESTERN'

CLIENT: MARINA CYCLERY
ART DIRECTOR/DESIGNER: GRANT PETERSON
COUNTRY: USA
INDUSTRY: BICYCLE STORE/FAHRRADGESCHÄFT/
MAGASIN DE CYCLES

CLIENT: CARAVAN

DESIGN FIRM: DAVID POWELL DESIGN

ART DIRECTOR/DESIGNER: DAVID POWELL

COUNTRY: USA

INDUSTRY: EXOTIC, HANDMADE GIFTS/

AUSGEFALLENE, HANDGEFERTIGTE GESCHENKARTIKEL/

ARTICLES CADEAU ORIGINAUX, FAITS À LA MAIN

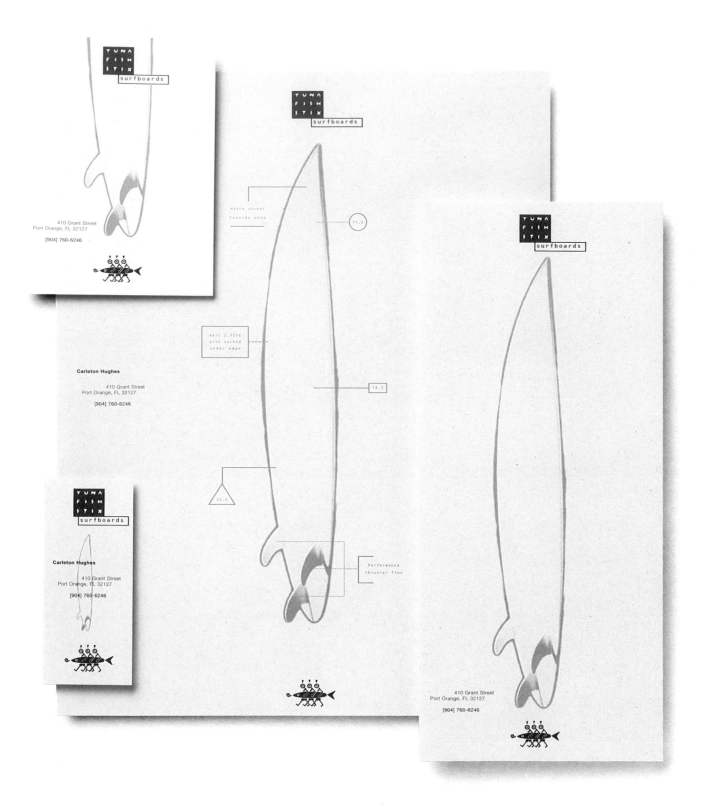

CLIENT: TUNA FISH STIX
DESIGN FIRM: HUGHES ADVERTISING INC.
CREATIVE DIRECTOR: RUDY FERNANDEZ
DESIGNER: TROY KING
PHOTOGRAPHER: DAVE KIESGAN
COUNTRY: USA
INDUSTRY: SURFBOARDS

BLUE SKY UNLIMITED

INTERACTIVE RETAILING
HEAR MUSIC, SMITH & HAWKEN, THE NATURE COMPANY, THE SCIENTIFIC REVOLUTION
8145 HOLTON DRIVE, FLORENCE, KENTUCKY 41042 TEL 606 342 7200 FAX 606 342 7202

CLIENT: BLUE SKY UNLIMITED
DESIGN FIRM: PENTAGRAM DESIGN
ART DIRECTOR: KIT HINRICHS
DESIGNER: JACKIE FOSHAUG
COUNTRY: USA
INDUSTRY: HOLDING COMPANY FOR RETAIL STORES/
HOLDING-GESELLSCHAFT FÜR LÄDEN/
SOCIÉTÉ HOLDING POUR LES DÉTAILLANTS

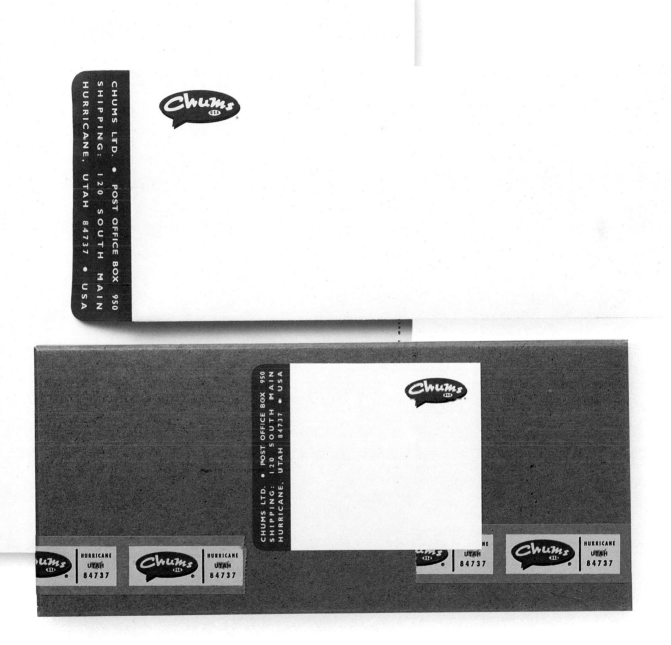

HELLOWEAR CLOTHING ● CHUMS RETENTION DEVICES ● CHUMS RESEARCH ● CHUMLEY'S CAFE

(THIS SPREAD)

CLIENT: CHUMS

DESIGN FIRM: DUFFY DESIGN

ART DIRECTOR: KOBE

DESIGNERS: KOBE, ALAN LEUSINK

COUNTRY: USA

INDUSTRY: RETAIL/EINZELHANDEL/COMMERCE DE DÉTAIL

(THIS PAGE) CLIENT: PROLER OEGGERLI DESIGN FIRM: RIGSBY DESIGN, INC. ART DIRECTOR: LANA RIGSBY DESIGNERS: LANA RIGSBY, MICHAEL THEDE ILLUSTRATOR: TROY S. FORD COUNTRY: USA INDUSTRY: ANTIQUE FURNISHINGS AND OBJECTS/ANTIQUITÄTEN/ANTIQUITÉS ■ (OPPOSITE PAGE) CLIENT: LAMALLE KITCHENWARE DESIGN FIRM: THE PUSHPIN GROUP ART DIRECTOR: SEYMOUR CHWAST DESIGNER: SEYMOUR CHWAST COUNTRY: USA INDUSTRY: KITCHENWARE IMPORTER & MANUFACTURER/HERSTELLER UND IMPORTEUR VON KÜCHENGERÄTEN/FABRICATION & IMPORT DE VAISSELLE

LAMALLE KITCHENWARE

Purveyors of Fine Cookware and Cutlery to Professional and Aspiring Chefs in Stellar Restaurants, Hotels, Clubs and Homes Across the Globe.

Copper and Stainless Steel Stovetop and Ovenware, Bakeware, Woodware, Pastry Tools, and Molds Retail and Wholesale Copper Retinned Bridal Registry

SINCE 1927
IMPORTERS & MANUFACTURERS

LAMALLE KITCHENWARE

36 West 25th Street
New York, NY 10010

Tel (212) 242-0750
Fax (212) 645-2996

SINCE 1927
IMPORTERS & MANUFACTURERS

JEAN TIBBETTS

LAMALLE KITCHENWARE

36 West 25th Street
New York, NY 10010

SINCE 1927
IMPORTERS & MANUFACTURERS

■ 36 WEST 25TH STREET, NEW YORK, NEW YORK 10010 ■ TELEPHONE: (212) 242-0750 FACSIMILE: (212) 645-2996 ■

Tower Letter [7] Designed for Tower Shop by NDC Graphics © 1994

Tower Letter [8] Designed for Tower Shop by NDC Graphics © 1994

(THIS SPREAD)

CLIENT: TOWER SHOP

DESIGN FIRM: NDC GRAPHICS INC.

ART DIRECTOR: KENZO NAKAGAWA

DESIGNERS: KENZO NAKAGAWA, HIROYASU NOBUYAMA, SATOSHI MORIKAMI

COUNTRY: JAPAN

INDUSTRY: SOUVENIR SHOP/MAGASIN DE SOUVENIRS

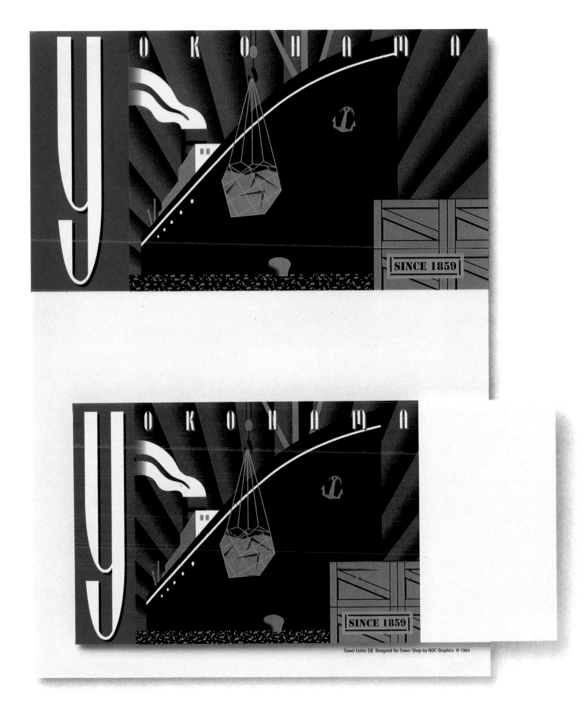

(THIS SPREAD)

CLIENT: TOWER SHOP

DESIGN FIRM: NDC GRAPHICS INC.

ART DIRECTOR: KENZO NAKAGAWA

DESIGNERS: KENZO NAKAGAWA, HIROYASU NOBUYAMA, SATOSHI MORIKAMI

COUNTRY: JAPAN

INDUSTRY: SOUVENIR SHOP/MAGASIN DE SOUVENIRS

CLIENT: THE JIMMIE HALE MISSION
DESIGN FIRM: DOGSTAR DESIGN
ART DIRECTOR: RALPH WATSON
DESIGNER/ILLUSTRATOR: RODNEY DAVIDSON
COUNTRY: USA
INDUSTRY: MISSION FOR THE HOMELESS/
OBDACHLOSENMISSION/
ASSOCIATION POUR LES SANS-ABRI

CLIENT: METRO QUEST PTY. LTD.

DESIGN FIRM: WATTS GRAPHIC DESIGN

ART DIRECTORS/DESIGNERS: PETER WATTS, HELEN WATTS

COUNTRY: AUSTRALIA

INDUSTRY: IMPORTER/IMPORTEUR

CLIENT: TIBET RUG COMPANY
DESIGN FIRM: ADRIAN PULFER DESIGN
ART DIRECTOR: ADRIAN PULFER
DESIGNERS: ADRIAN PULFER, JEFF STREEPER
ILLUSTRATOR: MARY JANE CALLISTER
COUNTRY: USA
INDUSTRY: RUG TRADE/TEPPICHHANDEL/COMMERCE DE TAPIS

CLIENT: THOMAS COOK TRAVELLERS CHEQUE
DESIGN FIRM: DESIGNWORKS
ART DIRECTOR/DESIGNER/ILLUSTRATOR: BILL CARDEN-HORTON
COUNTRY: NEW ZEALAND
INDUSTRY: TRAVEL AGENCY/REISEBÜRO/AGENCE DE TOURISME

Client: KINOS AARAU
Design Firm: WILD & FREY DESIGN
Art Director: HEINZ WILD
Designers: HEINZ WILD, MARIETTA ALBINUS
Country: SWITZERLAND
Industry: CINEMA/KINO/CINEMA

CLIENT: GRAND CENTRAL POST
DESIGN FIRM: PHOENIX CREATIVE
DESIGNER: ED MANTELS-SEEKER
ILLUSTRATOR: ARCHIVE, ED MANTELS-SEEKER
COUNTRY: USA
INDUSTRY: AUDIO & VIDEO POST PRODUCTION

Client: MARY CARBINE
Design Firm: 4TH PRIMARY
Designers: JOHN MARIN, MICHELE-HOAIDUC NGUYEN
Country: USA
Industry: FREELANCE FILM PRODUCTION/
FREIE FILMPRODUZENTIN/
PRODUCTRICE DE FILMS INDÉPENDANTE

CLIENT: LTV & COMPANY
DESIGN FIRM: TOLLESON DESIGN
ART DIRECTOR: STEVEN TOLLESON
DESIGNERS: STEVEN TOLLESON, CHASE WATTS
COUNTRY: USA
INDUSTRY: ENTERTAINMENT AND PRODUCTION COMPANY/
PRODUKTION VON FILMEN UND UNTERHALTUNGSSENDUNGEN/
PRODUCTION DE FILMS ET D'ÉMISSIONS DE DIVERTISSEMENT

C L I E N T : BEDFORD FALLS

D E S I G N F I R M : JAY VIGON STUDIO

A R T D I R E C T O R / D E S I G N E R : JAY VIGON

C O - D E S I G N E R / P R O D U C E R : CAROLINE PLASENCIA

P R I N T E R : DESIGN SOURCE

C O U N T R Y : USA

I N D U S T R Y : FILM COMPANY/FILMGFSELLSCHAFT/

COMPAGNIE CINÉMATOGRAPHIQUE

CLIENT: TIMES 3 PRODUCTIONS

DESIGN FIRM: GEER DESIGN, INC.

DESIGNER: MARK GEER

COUNTRY: USA

INDUSTRY: FILM PRODUCTION COMPANY/

FILMPRODUKTIONSGESELLSCHAFT/

SOCIÉTÉ DE PRODUCTION CINÉMATOGRAPHIQUE

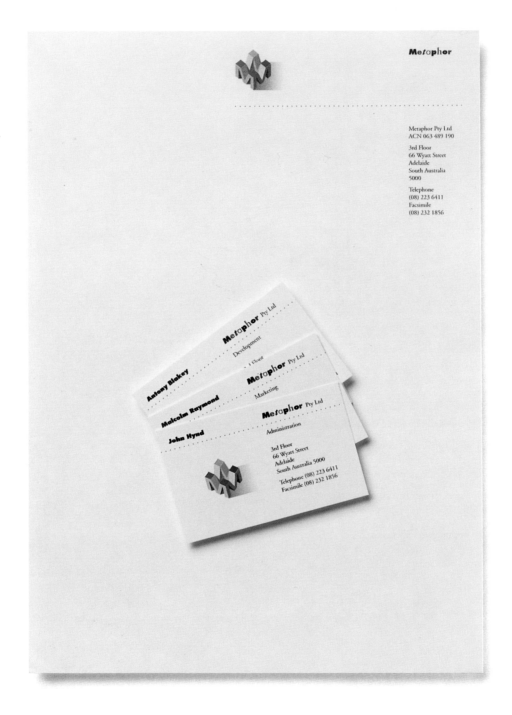

Client: METAPHOR PTY. LTD.

Design Firm: GRANT JORGENSEN GRAPHIC DESIGN

Art Director/Designer: GRANT JORGENSEN

Country: AUSTRALIA

Industry: MULTIMEDIA PRODUCTION/MULTIMEDIA-PRODUKTIONEN/

PRODUCTIONS MULTIMÉDIA

10 Hill Street • Mill Valley, California 94941
800-815-1234

10 Hill Street • Mill Valley, California 94941

10 Hill Street • Mill Valley, California 94941

Kathleen Mapel

10 Hill Street
Mill Valley, California
94941

800-815-1234

CLIENT: FIREDOG PICTURES
DESIGN FIRM: LISA LEVIN DESIGN
ART DIRECTOR: LISA LEVIN
DESIGNERS: LISA LEVIN, JILL JACOBSON
ILLUSTRATOR: MICHAEL SCHWAB
COUNTRY: USA
INDUSTRY: PRODUCTION OF CHILDREN'S VIDEOS/
HERSTELLUNG VON VIDEOS FÜR KINDER/
PRODUCTION DE VIDÉOS POUR ENFANTS

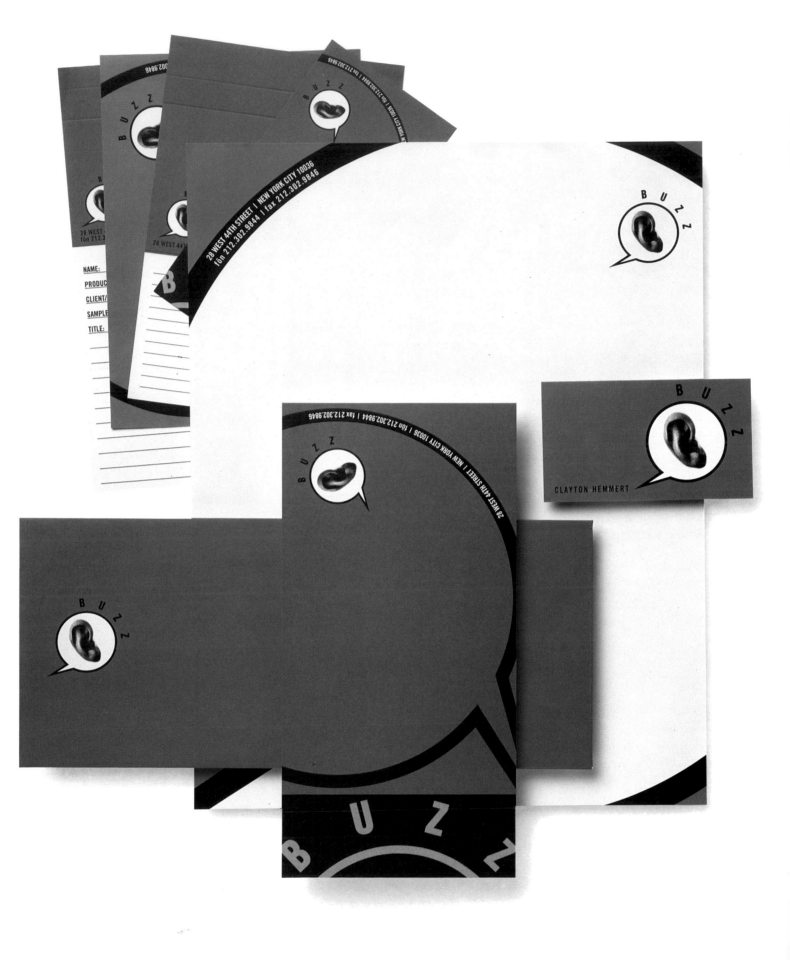

(THIS SPREAD)

CLIENT: BUZZ

DESIGN FIRM: FULL CIRCLE STUDIO

ART DIRECTOR/DESIGNER/ILLUSTRATOR: KENNY DUGGAN

COUNTRY: USA

INDUSTRY: AUDIO & VIDEO

CLIENT: BUZZ
DESIGN FIRM: FULL CIRCLE STUDIO
ART DIRECTOR/DESIGNER/ILLUSTRATOR: KENNY DUGGAN
COUNTRY: USA
INDUSTRY: SOUND CREATION AND EDITING (AUDIO/VIDEO)/
TONSTUDIO (AUDIO/VIDEO)/
STUDIO D'ENREGISTREMENT (AUDIO/VIDÉO)

CLIENT: TWO WAY TV

DESIGN FIRM: TUTSSELS

ART DIRECTOR: GLENN TUTSSEL

DESIGNERS: GLENN TUTSSEL, GARY HOLT

COUNTRY: GREAT BRITAIN

INDUSTRY: INTERACTIVE TV/INTERAKTIVES FERNSEHEN/
TV INTERACTIVE

BLOODSTONE PICTURES
2426 BARTLETT, NUMBER 2
HOUSTON, TEXAS 77098
TELEPHONE 713-526-9636
FACSIMILE 713-526-6214

CLIENT: BLOODSTONE PICTURES
DESIGN FIRM: RIGSBY DESIGN, INC.
ART DIRECTOR: LANA RIGSBY
DESIGNERS: LANA RIGSBY, MICHAEL THEDE
ILLUSTRATOR: TROY S. FORD
COUNTRY: USA
INDUSTRY: FILM PRODUCTION COMPANY/FILMPRODUKTIONSGESELLSCHAFT/
SOCIÉTÉ DE PRODUCTION CINÉMATOGRAPHIQUE

CLIENT: WALSH CINEMATOGRAPHY INC.

DESIGN FIRM: DESIGN SERVICES INC.

ART DIRECTORS: ROD PARKER, TIM HOPE

ILLUSTRATOR: TIM HOPE

COUNTRY: USA

INDUSTRY: CINEMATOGRAPHY/

FILMAUFNAHMESTUDIO/

STUDIO D'ENREGISTREMENTS DE FILMS

CLIENT: SAN FRANCISCO FILM SOCIETY
DESIGN FIRM: PRIMO ANGELI INC.
ART DIRECTORS: CARLO PAGODA, PRIMO ANGELI
DESIGNERS: MARCELO DE FREITAS, PAUL TERRILL, PRIMO ANGELI
PRODUCTION MANAGER: ERIC KUBLY
COUNTRY: USA
INDUSTRY: FILM SOCIETY/FILMCLUB/SOCIÉTÉ CINÉMATOGRAPHIQUE

CLIENT: CINETEAM COMMERCIALS BV.

DESIGN FIRM/ART DIRECTOR/DESIGNER: KOEWEIDEN/POSTMA

COUNTRY: NETHERLANDS

INDUSTRY: COMMERCIALS PRODUCTION/WERBESPOTPRODUKTION/

PRODUCTION DE SPOTS PUBLICITAIRES

CLIENT: TURNER ENTERTAINMENT
DESIGN FIRM: CHARLES S. ANDERSON DESIGN COMPANY
ART DIRECTOR: CHARLES S. ANDERSON
DESIGNERS: CHARLES S. ANDERSON, PAUL HOWART, JOEL TEMPLIN
COUNTRY: USA
INDUSTRY: ENTERTAINMENT CONGLOMORATE/UNTERHALTUNGSKONGLOMERAT/INDUSTRIE DU DIVERTISSEMENT

San Francisco Production Group   phone: (415) 495.5595
550 Bryant St., San Francisco, CA 94107   fax: (415) 543.8370

San Francisco
Production Group
550 Bryant Street
San Francisco, CA 94107

550 Bryant Street
San Francisco, CA 94107
phone: (415) 495.5595
fax: (415) 543.8370

CLIENT: SAN FRANCISCO PRODUCTION GROUP
DESIGN FIRM: MORLA DESIGN
ART DIRECTOR: JENNIFER MORLA
DESIGNERS: JENNIFER MORLA, CRAIG BAILEY
PHOTOGRAPHER: BETTMAN ARCHIVE
PHOTO IMAGING: MARK EASTMAN
COUNTRY: USA
INDUSTRY: VIDEO PRODUCTION FACILITY/
VIDEOPRODUKTIONSSTUDIO/
STUDIO DE PRODUCTION DE VIDÉOS

CLIENT: WIRE TV

DESIGN FIRM: TUTSSELS

ART DIRECTOR: GLENN TUTSSEL

DESIGNERS: GLENN TUTSSEL, TIM GREY

ILLUSTRATOR: COLIN FREWIN

COUNTRY: GREAT BRITAIN

INDUSTRY: PRIVATE TV/PRIVATFERNSEHEN/CHAÎNE PRIVÉE

CLIENT: MEGAFON DESIGN

DESIGN FIRM/ART DIRECTOR/DESIGNER/ILLUSTRATOR: MEGAFON DESIGN

COUNTRY: NORWAY

INDUSTRY: DESIGN & FILM

CLIENT: MARY WOODS

DESIGN FIRM: SWIETER DESIGN UNITED STATES

ART DIRECTOR: JOHN SWIETER

DESIGNERS: JOHN SWIETER, PAUL MUNSTERMAN, MARK FORD

COUNTRY: USA

INDUSTRY: COPYWRITER/TEXTEHIN/

RÉDACTRICE PUBLICITAIRE

INDEX

VERZEICHNIS

INDEX

. . . .

DESIGN FIRMS

. . . .

CALL FOR ENTRIES

EINLADUNG

APPEL D'ENVOIS

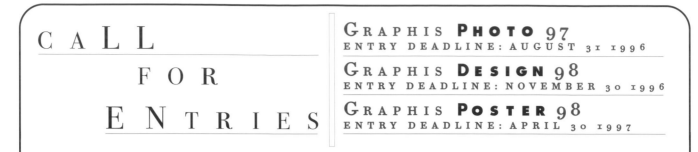

C A L L

F O R

E N T R I E S

GRAPHIS **PHOTO** 97
ENTRY DEADLINE: AUGUST 31 1996

GRAPHIS **DESIGN** 98
ENTRY DEADLINE: NOVEMBER 30 1996

GRAPHIS **POSTER** 98
ENTRY DEADLINE: APRIL 30 1997

Graphis Photo 97 (Entry Deadline: August 31, 1996)

■ Ads, catalogs, invitations, announcements, record covers, and calendars on any subject. Photographs taken for consumer or trade magazines, newspapers, books and corporate publications. Personal studies on any subject. Experimental or student work on any subject. Eligibility: All work produced between September 1995 and August 1996. ● Anzeigen, Kataloge, Plattenhüllen, Kalender. Photos für Zeitschriften, Zeitungen, Bücher und Firmenpublikationen. Persönliche Studien. Experimentelle Aufnahmen oder Studentenarbeiten. In Frage kommen: Arbeiten, die zwischen September 1995 und August 1996 entstanden sind. ▲ Publicité, catalogues, invitations, annonces, pochettes de disques, calendriers. Reportages pour magazines et journaux, livres et publications d'entreprise. Études personnelles, créations expérimentales ou projets d'étudiants. Seront admis: tous les travaux réalisés entre septembre 1995 et août 1996.

Graphis Design 98 (Entry Deadline: November 30, 1996)

■ Ads; promotion brochures, catalogs, invitations, record covers, announcements, logos, corporate campaigns, calendars, books, book covers, packaging, company magazines; newspapers, consumer or trade magazines, annual reports; illustration. Eligibility: All work produced between December 1995 and November 1996. ● Werbung, Broschüren, Kataloge, Plattenhüllen, Logos, Firmenkampagnen, Kalender, Bücher, Buchumschläge, Packungen. Zeitschriften, Hauszeitschriften, Jahresberichte, Illustrationen. In Frage kommen: Arbeiten, die zwischen Dezember 1995 und November 1996 entstanden sind. ▲ Publicité; brochures, catalogues, invitations, pochettes de disques, annonces, logos, identité visuelle, calendriers, livres, packaging; journaux, revues, magazines de sociétés, rapports annuels; illustration. Seront admis: les travaux réalisés entre décembre 1995 et novembre 1996.

Graphis Poster 98 (Entry Deadline: April 30, 1997)

■ Advertising, cultural, and social posters. Eligibility: All work produced between May 1996 and April 1997. ● Plakate für Werbezwecke sowie kulturelle und soziale Plakate. In Frage kommen: Arbeiten, die zwischen Mai 1996 und April 1997 entstanden sind. ▲ Affiches publicitaires, culturelles et sociales. Seront admis: tous les travaux réalisés entre mai 1996 et avril 1997.

■ **What to send:** Reproduction-quality duplicate transparencies (4x5″ or 35mm). They are required for large, bulky or valuable pieces. ALL 35MM SLIDES MUST BE CARDBOARD-MOUNTED, NO GLASS SLIDE MOUNTS PLEASE! *Please mark the transparencies with your name.* If you do send printed pieces they should be unmounted. WE REGRET THAT ENTRIES CANNOT BE RETURNED. ● **Was einsenden:** Wenn immer möglich, schicken Sie uns bitte reproduktionsfähige Duplikatdias. *Bitte Dias mit Ihrem Namen versehen..* Bitte schicken Sie auf keinen Fall Originaldias. KLEINBILDDIAS BITTE IM KARTONRAHMEN, KEIN GLAS! Falls Sie uns das gedruckte Beispiel schicken, bitten wir Sie, dieses gut geschützt aber nicht aufgezogen zu senden. WIR BEDAUERN, DASS EINSENDUNGEN NICHT ZURÜCKGESCHICKT WERDEN KÖNNEN. ▲ **Que nous envoyer:** Nous vous recommandons de nous faire parvenir de préférence des duplicata de diapositives (4x5″ ou 35mm. N'oubliez pas d'inscrire votre nom dessus). NE PAS ENVOYER DE DIAPOSITIVES SOUS VERRE! Si vous désirez envoyer des travaux imprimés, protégez-les, mais ne les montez pas sur carton. NOUS VOUS SIGNALONS QUE LES ENVOIS QUE VOUS NOUS AUREZ FAIT PARVENIR NE POURRONT VOUS ÊTRE RETOURNÉS.

■ **How to package your entry:** Please tape (do not glue) the completed entry form (or a copy) to the back of each piece. Please do not send anything by air freight. Write "No Commercial Value" on the package, and label it "Art for Contest." ● Wie und wohin senden: Bitte befestigen Sie das ausgefüllte Einsendeetikett (oder eine Kopie davon) mit Klebstreifen (nicht kleben) auf jeder Arbeit und legen Sie noch ein Doppel davon lose bei. Bitte auf keinen Fall Luft- oder Bahnfracht senden. Deklarieren Sie «Ohne jeden Handelswert» und «Arbeitsproben für Wettbewerb». ▲ Comment préparer votre envoi: Veuillez scotcher (ne pas coller) au dos de chaque spécimen les étiquettes dûment remplies. Nous vous prions également de faire un double de chaque étiquette, que vous joindrez à votre envoi, mais sans le coller ou le fixer. Ne nous expédiez rien en fret aérien. Indiquez «Sans aucune valeur commerciale» et «Echantillons pour concours».

■ **Entry fees:** Single entries: North America US$25; Germany DM 25,00; all other countries SFr 25.00. Three or more pieces entered in a single contest: North America US$65, Germany DM 65,00; all other countries SFr 65.00. **Students entry fees** (please send copy of student identification): US$15 for each single entry, US$35 for each campaign or series of three or more pieces entered in a single contest. ● **Einsendegebühren:** Für jede einzelne Arbeit: DM 25,00/SFr 25.00. Für jede Kampagne oder Serie von drei oder mehr Stück: DM 65,00/SFr 65.00. **Einsendegebühren für Studenten** (Ausweiskopie mitschicken): Für jede einzelne Arbeit: DM 15,00/SFr 15.00. Für jede Kampagne oder Serie von drei oder mehr Stück: DM 35,00/SFr 35.00. ▲ **Droits d'admission:** Envoi d'un seul travail: US$ 25/SFr. 25.00. Campagne ou série de trois travaux ou plus pour un seul concours: US$ 65/SFr. 65.00. **Droits d'admission pour étudiants** (veuillez envoyer une photocopie de la carte d'étudiant): US$15/SFr. 15.00 pour un seul travail, $35/SFr. 35 pour chaque série de trois travaux ou plus.

■ **Where to send:** Entries from North America and Canada should be sent to the New York office and checks should be made payable to GRAPHIS US, INC, NEW YORK. Entries from all other countries should be sent to the Zurich office and checks should be made payable to GRAPHIS PRESS CORP., ZURICH. ● **Wohin senden:** Bitte senden Sie uns Ihre Arbeiten an Graphis Zürich zusammen mit einem Scheck, ausgestellt in SFr. (auf eine Schweizer Bank ziehen oder Eurocheck) oder überweisen Sie den Betrag auf PC Luzern 60-3520-6 oder PSchK Frankfurt 3000 57-602 (BLZ 50010060). ▲ **Où envoyer:** Veuillez envoyer vos travaux à Graphis Zurich et joindre un chèque tiré sur une banque suisse ou un Eurochèque; ou verser le montant sur le compte chèque postal Lucerne 60-3520-6.

GRAPHIS PRESS, DUFOURSTRASSE 107, CH-8008 ZÜRICH, SWITZERLAND, TELEPHONE: 41-1-383 82 11, FAX: 41-1-383 16 43
GRAPHIS US, INC., 141 LEXINGTON AVENUE, NEW YORK, NY 10016, TELEPHONE: (212) 532 9387, FAX: (212) 213 3229

ENTRY FORMS

GRAPHIS **PHOTO** 97
ENTRY DEADLINE: AUGUST 31 1996

GRAPHIS **DESIGN** 98
ENTRY DEADLINE: NOVEMBER 30 1996

GRAPHIS **POSTER** 98
ENTRY DEADLINE: APRIL 30 1997

I WISH TO ENTER THE ATTACHED IN THE FOLLOWING GRAPHIS COMPETITION:

☐ **GRAPHIS POSTER** 98 (APRIL 30, 1997)

CATEGORY CODES
PO1   ADVERTISING
PO2   PROMOTIONAL
PO3   CULTURE
PO4   SOCIAL

☐ **GRAPHIS PHOTO** 97 (AUGUST 31, 1996)

CATEGORY CODES
PH1   FASHION
PH2   JOURNALISM
PH3   STILL LIFE
PH4   FOOD
PH5   PEOPLE
PH6   PRODUCTS
PH7   LANDSCAPES
PH8   ARCHITECTURE
PH9   WILD LIFE
PH10 SPORTS
PH11 FINE ART

☐ **GRAPHIS DESIGN** 98 (NOVEMBER 30, 1996)

CATEGORY CODES
DE1   BROCHURES
DE2   EDITORIAL
DE3   ILLUSTRATION
DE4   CORPORATE IDENTITY
DE5   PACKAGING
DE6   CALENDARS
DE7   CD/RECORD COVERS
DE8   BOOKS
DE9   MULTIMEDIA
DE10 MISCELLANEOUS

SENDER: _____   CATEGORY CODE: _____

COMPANY _____

STREET _____

CITY/STATE _____   ZIP/COUNTRY _____

TELEPHONE _____   FAX _____

ART DIRECTOR: _____

COMPANY _____

STREET _____

CITY/STATE _____   ZIP/COUNTRY _____

TELEPHONE _____   FAX _____

DESIGNER: _____

COMPANY _____

STREET _____

CITY/STATE _____   ZIP/COUNTRY _____

TELEPHONE _____   FAX _____

PHOTOGRAPHER/ILLUSTRATOR: _____

STREET _____

CITY/STATE _____   ZIP/COUNTRY _____

TELEPHONE _____   FAX _____

DESIGN FIRM: _____

STREET _____

CITY/STATE _____   ZIP/COUNTRY _____

TELEPHONE _____   FAX _____

CLIENT: _____

STREET _____

CITY/STATE _____   ZIP/COUNTRY _____

TELEPHONE _____   FAX _____

I HEREBY GRANT PERMISSION FOR THE ATTACHED MATERIAL TO BE PUBLISHED FREE OF CHARGE IN ANY GRAPHIS BOOK, ARTICLE IN GRAPHIS MAGAZINE, OR ANY ADVERTISEMENT, BROCHURE OR OTHER MATERIAL PRODUCED FOR THE PURPOSE OF PROMOTING GRAPHIS PUBLICATIONS.

SIGNATURE _____   DATE _____

GRAPHIS PRESS, DUFOURSTRASSE 107, CH-8008 ZÜRICH, SWITZERLAND, TELEPHONE: 41-1-383 82 11, FAX: 41-1-383 16 43

GRAPHIS US, INC., 141 LEXINGTON AVENUE, NEW YORK, NY 10016, TELEPHONE: (212) 532 9387, FAX: (212) 213 3229

Graphis 296

Graphis 296

The Digital Revolution: R/GA Softimage Silicon Graphics European Mindscapes Multimedia

Graphis 295

Graphis 295

Carson Chiat/Day Apeloig Leith Agency Legorreta Gorham

Graphis 297

Ishioka Fletcher Arnell ABV Achilli & Piazza CD Boxed Sets

G R A P H I S   M A G A Z I N E

SUBSCRIBE TO GRAPHIS: USA, CANADA, SOUTH AMERICA, ASIA

MAGAZINE	USA	CANADA	SOUTHAMERICA/ ASIA/PACIFIC
☐ ONE YEAR (6 ISSUES)	US$ 89.00	US$ 99.00	US$ 125.00
☐ TWO YEARS (12 ISSUES)	US$ 159.00	US$ 179.00	US$ 235.00
☐ AIRMAIL SURCHARGE (6 ISSUES)	US$ 59.00	US$ 59.00	US$ 59.00

☐ 25% DISCOUNT FOR STUDENTS WITH COPY OF VALID,
DATED STUDENT ID AND PAYMENT WITH ORDER

☐ CHECK ENCLOSED

USE CREDIT CARDS (DEBITED IN US DOLLARS)

☐ AMERICAN EXPRESS

☐ MASTERCARD

☐ VISA

CARD NO.   EXP. DATE

CARDHOLDER NAME

SIGNATURE

☐ PLEASE BILL ME

(PLEASE PRINT)

NAME

TITLE

COMPANY

ADDRESS

CITY

STATE/PROVINCE   ZIP CODE

COUNTRY

SEND ORDER FORM AND MAKE CHECK PAYABLE TO:
GRAPHIS US, INC.,
141 LEXINGTON AVENUE,
NEW YORK, NY 10016-8193, USA

SERVICE BEGINS WITH ISSUE THAT IS CURRENT WHEN
ORDER IS PROCESSED.   (C9B0A)

SUBSCRIBE TO GRAPHIS: EUROPE, AFRICA, MIDDLE EAST

MAGAZINE	EUROPE/AFRICA MIDDLE EAST	GERMANY	U.K.
☐ ONE YEAR (6 ISSUES)	SFR. 164.–	DM 190,–	£ 68.00
☐ TWO YEARS (12 ISSUES)	SFR. 295.–	DM 342,–	£ 122.00
☐ AIRMAIL SURCHARGES	SFR 65.–	DM 75,–	£ 30.00
☐ REGISTERED MAIL	SFR 20.–	DM 24,–	£ 9.00

☐ CHECK ENCLOSED (PLEASE MAKE SFR.–CHECK PAYABLE TO
A SWISS BANK)

☐ STUDENTS MAY REQUEST A 25% DISCOUNT BY SENDING
STUDENT ID

FOR CREDIT CARD PAYMENT (ALL CARDS DEBITED IN SWISS
FRANCS):

☐ AMERICAN EXPRESS   ☐ DINER'S CLUB

☐ VISA/BARCLAYCARD/CARTE BLEUE

CARD NO.   EXP. DATE

CARDHOLDER NAME

SIGNATURE

☐ PLEASE BILL ME

(PLEASE PRINT)

LAST NAME

FIRST NAME

TITLE

COMPANY

ADDRESS

CITY   POSTAL CODE

COUNTRY

NOTE TO GERMAN SUBSCRIBERS ONLY:
ICH ERKLÄRE MICH EINVERSTANDEN, DASS MEINE NEUE
ADRESSE DURCH DIE POST AN DEN VERTRIEB WEITERGELEITET
WIRD.

PLEASE SEND ORDER FORM AND MAKE CHECK PAYABLE TO:
GRAPHIS PRESS CORP.
DUFOURSTRASSE 107
CH–8008 ZÜRICH, SWITZERLAND

SERVICE BEGINS WITH ISSUE THAT IS CURRENT WHEN
ORDER IS PROCESSED.   (C9B0A)

D0687630

Chateau, Jardin, Cuisine

Chateau, Jardin, Cuisine

Secret Recipes from the Ardèche

REGINA VON PLANTA

UNICORN

International celebrity chef Reza Mahammad has created his own brand of style and design to Indian cooking. He has written two books and has been a presenter and star in several notable UK television programs including a groundbreaking documentary series filmed with Claudio von Planta. In addition Reza oversees the management of the family restaurant, the famous Star of India in South Kensington, London. His latest venture is a cookery school near Bordeaux in France, where fine Indian cooking is combined with Middle Eastern influence, Mediterranean flavours and local ingredients to create a fresh new style he has aptly named 'Frindian'.

Chateau, Jardin, Cuisine

Over many years I have witnessed first hand Regina von Planta's boundless energy, enthusiasm and dedication in the Ardeche. She has created an extraordinary life for her family and herself in this stunning and remote village near Largentiere, located in the narrow valley of the river Ligne.

In this wild landscape of gorges and rugged mountainous valleys Regina's adventure began. She left behind the city life, bought a small farmhouse with her husband, Claudio and joined the local community by picking up a garden trowel. She learned all aspects of this extraordinarily rich culture with its surprising culinary treats. This book describes Regina's journey with her many challenges of the terrain as she learned all she could about local traditional recipes using produce from the land.

This is a book for home cooks. The recipes are simple and clear enough for novice chefs yet unique enough to tantalize even the most discerning experts in the kitchen. Most of the dishes are homely and may seem to be humble but the end results capture the spirit of the landscape with meals that thrill the tastebuds. Truly, the enclosed recipes create exquisite dining.

Reza Mahammad

> *"I learned how to live away from the city and traded my high heels for muddy boots and a garden trowel"*

Foreword

Fifteen years ago, my husband and I, through extraordinary good fortune, found and purchased a beautiful but rundown small farm in a remote region of France. Soon we set out with a car, stuffed with things we no longer needed in London, plus our two daughters, to spend our first summer in the Ardèche. Those weeks turned into a year and then two years. As our girls learned a new language and the French way of life, I learned how to live away from the city and traded my high heels for muddy boots and a garden trowel. It is an adventure that continues to this day and has inspired me in ways I would never have imagined.

It was the neglected land that drew me in: the many terraces descending towards a small river, covered with pine trees, semi-dry water wells and bramble. I dreamt of transforming this dying overgrown ruin of a farm into a garden. I made mistake after mistake after mistake. Finally, I learned to respect the land and its terrain, understand the soil and, most importantly how to best use our natural supply of water. It took a very long time but eventually I lost my romantic illusions and understood what the locals already knew: life on this land can be hard but also very rewarding. Everything people did had a purpose and it was all connected to their land.

My semi successful efforts to preserve our many crumbling terraces, to prune old fruit trees and to introduce new plants, led to grudging respect. Soon, our neighbours asked if they could use our cherries, quinces, walnuts and our water. In return they gave us quince paste, chestnut cream and Vin de Noix. I realised how imaginatively the local produce was used, how the many family rituals were linked to the local cuisine and how strongly everyone was attached to the 'terroir', their countryside. As a sideline, some wine growers would replant old vines and, thus, some forgotten and sometimes forbidden wines made a comeback. We tasted them during those long 'aperitifs dînatoirs,' and it was there that I became intrigued by how people live, cook and think. Nathalie Jacques, now a close friend, mentioned that her mother has vast knowledge of all the traditional recipes. When I first met Mado Jaques, she stated with genuine modesty that she knew everything 'autour du cochon'. At that very moment the idea of writing this book was born.

I asked everyone, who was willing to share his or her knowledge about Ardèche cooking, to make some special dishes. Then I convinced this private community to let me be a witness with my camera. Later, I realized that we had no vegetarian dishes because, traditionally, the cuisine is centred on pork. Also, there were hardly any fish dishes, because many of the rivers no longer contain enough fish. Fishing has become a sport and fishermen do not provide their families as before. As you will see, we filled those gaps.

I feel most fortunate that my friends shared with me some of their favorite memories and secrets of this out of the way region. Maybe they shared because I, a foreigner, was so deeply interested in the complex challenges of their unique rural lifestyle. I find it even more fascinating to see how this traditional cuisine is reinventing itself.

The amazing and productive friendship with Guillemette Aubry, who lives the extremes of town and country between Paris and St.Michel de Boulogne, developed out of this great adventure. Whether rooted in the Ardèche or more loosely connected to this beautiful country, two things unite all the cooks who gave so generously with their heart, their spirits and their time: the hope that these very personal recipes might not be forgotten and possibly inspire others to experiment with new ideas and ingredients.

Regina von Planta

Dedications

t is the local people who make a place become truly special, a place that resonates within your heart and inspires the spirit. For me, that place is here in the Mas Saint Esprit. I would like to dedicate this book to the friends and neighbours who gave much time and energy to share their extensive knowledge.

Guillemette Aubry, Mado Jacques, Simone Reynouard, Marie Christine and Eric Heyraud, Nathalie Jacques and Bruno Lebrun and 'Nada' Georges Audo are passionate cooks who, with their favourite recipes, have made this book. In addition, Guillemette helped me with translating the English texts into correct French, which was hugely helpful.

Also, I would like to thank all our neighbours and friends in Largentière and the Mas St.Esprit, in particular Françoise and Claude Blanc, Serge and Christine Tachon, Christine and Jean-Yves Rue-Fenouche, Isabelle Lepvrier, Sylvie and Daniel Dupont, who gave me much invaluable advice. And I will never forget my visit to the farm of Marie Josée and Claude Smets, who took great care when introducing me to the delicate art of cheese making. I have a special note of thanks to Michael Jack, a consultant who taught me about the conservation of jams, jellies and condiments. He made helpful and, to his mind, life-preserving comments on food safety.

This book would never have come into existence without Jonathan Richards, who produced it, and it was Mark Kensett, who was kind enough to improve my photographs. Kim Carpenter edited the book. She is a generous friend but quite severe when it comes to the use of the English language. She is American and a television writer/producer, which might explain why she found it unimaginable that we use the word carcass in connection with fine dining.

Finally, I would like to thank my husband, Claudio, and my two daughters Larissa and Xenia, who never complained while I experimented with all these wonderful recipes.

About Us

From left to right: Bruno, Regina, Simone, Guillemette, Mado, Natalie, Marie Christine and Eric

Guillemette

Guillemette Aubry is an inspirational cook. She fuses culinary elements from Asia and Africa with Ardèche cooking. She cooks for her extended family at the Château de Boulogne and frequently adds new elements to her recipes. In this book she shares some of her favourite ones with us although for Guillemette cooking is always a work in progress.

Mado and Simone

Mado Jacques and Simone Reynouard are sisters. Their entire family is renowned for their extensive knowledge of the traditional ways of life and of cooking. They come from a farming family and are aware that this traditional way of living and the knowledge of how to make things is going to disappear in the Ardèche. Mado says that she is good at anything to do with pork, others agree that is a massive understatement. For her, the main point of this little book is that her recipes won't be forgotten. Simone is the custodian of L'Abeille, which originally grew and raised silk worms, sheep, oxen and goats and now has been restored with exactly the same love for this way of life. It was her idea to make our bread in the old oven in one of the courtyards of this beautiful farm.

Natalie and Bruno

Nathalie Jacques and Bruno Lebrun live with their children in the hills above Largentière where Bruno plants saffron on the terraces above their home as part of his project on biological farming. The project has inspired him to create recipes for the saffron's many uses. Nathalie is Mado's daughter. She is an artist and an art therapist. She relishes cooking for large numbers of people and each time to come up with inspired recipes. She also makes hundreds of pots of jam with saffron, which Bruno then sells on the farmer's market in Ruoms.

Marie and Eric

Marie Christine and Eric Heyraud live in the hills above Vals les Bains. Up there one finds sheep, rabbits, mushrooms, chestnuts and a vegetable garden. Although their work takes them to an office every day, Marie Christine and Eric's true passion is to preserve the rich heritage of the Ardèche. Together they made the decision to live in a sustainable fashion and to take care of their land. The nearest supermarket is far away on a truly challenging road. This might explain their three huge freezers, packed with coulis, meat, confits and mushrooms, and their cellars full of wine, sausages and jams. All of this is how they create their culinary paradise.

Regina

Regina von Planta is in the process of creating a garden near Largentière. The difficult terrain has made her realise the varied and extensive skills that are required to live off the land. It is a way of life that is disappearing. So she was intrigued to learn how these skills have evolved into producing excellent food. There is no shortage of books on Ardèche cooking, but her interest has been inspired by these amazing personalities. She is the editor of this recipe collection.

Recipes

1. Orange Wine

One of the best 'infused aperitifs' I have experienced in the Ardèche is this Orange Wine. One drinks it almost too easily and it should be served in moderation and enjoyed at a leisurely pace. Marie Christine and Eric make it every winter when the bitter Seville oranges are juicy and in season. You can consume this wine fresh or after a couple of months. It lasts up to 2 years, when it takes the flavour of a fortified wine called 'vin cuit'.

5 litres white wine (such as Chardonnay)
3 Seville oranges, unwaxed
1 Lemon
1 Vanilla pod
1 Cinnamon stick
1 kg Granulated sugar
4 Whole cloves
½ litre Eau de vie of fruit with 50° alcohol
Glass container of 10 litres with an airtight closure.

Wash the fruit, cut in quarters and take out the pips.

Pour the white wine into the glass container. Add the sugar and mix well. Add the eau de vie and stir again. Put the cinnamon, the vanilla, the cloves, the oranges and the lemon into the mixture.

Leave to macerate for 40 days in a dark and cool place and regularly give it a little shake. At the end of the process, take out the fruit and the spices. Pass the wine through a triple cloth and if it is still cloudy then pass it through a coffee filter. Divide between bottles, seal and let it mature for another month or so.

Use a funnel and coffee filters to filter the orange wine. You might have to do it two or three times so that the liquid is clear. Sealing bottles: you can use any size or variety of bottles you like. If you are able to seal it completely with a cork then this wine can be kept in a cool place for several years. However, most people never keep it long enough to really find out. In case you are using resealable bottles, then it will keep for up to a year in a fridge or a very cool basement.

Serve really cool without ice cubes and decorate with orange slices.

2. Le Guignolet

Not only does the Guignolet have a beautiful ruby colour, it is also a fresh and fruity aperitif made with ripe but sour cherries. It takes its name from the 'guigne', a cherry which is widely grown in Anjou, where this liqueur was created by a nun in the 17th century. Other cherries, such as the 'marasque' and the 'griotte' make an equally delicious Guignolet. Once the cherries have been macerated for 40 days in alcohol and sugar, the alcohol level is about 16° to 18°.

400g cherries 'griottes'
5 litres good red wine
800g sugar
1 vanilla pod
½ litre alcohol 60°

Take a large earthenware jar and put in the vanilla pod, the alcohol and the sugar. Stir well and add the wine. Pour in the cherries with their stones and stir the mixture thoroughly. Leave the jar for 40 days in a cool place, such as a cellar to macerate. During that time stir it about once a week. Afterwards, filter and preserve the Guignolet in bottles.

Serve this aperitif without ice. There are those who add Kirsch, Gin or Vodka to it, but you can also create an interesting cocktail by adding cherry nectar and champagne.

3. Dip with Fresh Goat Cheese

Nearly everyone is able to whip up an interesting dip and we asked ourselves whether there should be one in this book. However, this dip is particularly delicious.

100g goat cheese, as fresh as possible
125g full fat yoghurt. For this recipe we used yoghurt from the 'Ferme de Huédous' in the Ardèche.
½ charlotte, or spring onions or even a small onion,
Herbs: mint, chives and/or parsley, rosemary – powdered if available.
A little salt and pepper

To accompany this dip, make small pieces of toasted corn bread and cut batons of raw carrots and beetroots – maybe use cocktail sticks to avoid staining your fingers. You can also serve it with raw cauliflower or cucumber. Generally, let yourself be inspired by the contents of your fridge and whatever is in season.

4. Dip with Herbs

The recipe for this classic herb sauce, which contains masses of at least 6 different herbs is very close to the German 'Grüne Sauce' or Green Sauce, which is a speciality in Hessen and used to be one of Goethe's favourite dishes. Its season starts in spring when the fresh herbs have the finest taste. This traditional sauce has also given its name to Maundy Thursday, called Grundonnerstag in German.

125g mayonnaise, preferably homemade
4 hard-boiled eggs
Salt and Pepper
5 tbs vegetable oil
Herbs: fresh parsley, sorrel or cress, chervil, tarragon, chives and/or spring onion, mint (not too much), and possibly a bit of fresh coriander
5 small gherkins
1 grated lemon rind

Mash up the egg yolks, mix in the oil and the lemon rind; add the mayonnaise until you get a smooth sauce. Then add the egg whites cut into tiny pieces and finally the herbs, which you have cut very thinly. This is better than to make the sauce in a blender because it preserves the fine taste of the herbs. Be generous and choose the proportions according to your taste. Traditionally not one of the herbs has more than 30 percent of the mix. The green sauce is served cold and together with boiled new potatoes it makes a whole meal. Otherwise the sauce is an excellent accompaniment to roast beef or fish.

5. Red Pepper Dip

This sauce is an interesting 'dip' for an aperitif served with cucumber sticks, new potatoes, grilled aubergines, small toasts. However, it is also a delicious sauce for flat pasta such as tagliatelle.

6 red peppers
2 onions
2 garlic cloves
Olive oil or peanut oil or sunflower oil
Herbes de Provence
Salt and pepper

To peel the red peppers, make your life a easy, and put them in a very hot oven or even under a grill turning them occasionally. The skin should get quite black and dry. Then you can either throw them into very cold water or put them directly from the oven into a plastic bag. Close it well and wait for about half an hour and the skin should come off easily.

Brown the onions and the garlic in the peanut oil, which works best for this purpose; add the peppers which you chopped into small pieces; salt, pepper and herbs; and cook over medium heat, stirring gently from time to time. Put the mixture in a blender adding 1 to 2 tablespoons of olive oil.

6. Trout Mousse

Trout in the many rivers of the Adèche is an ancient tradition and a modern sport. However, there are several farms to serve the increasing demand.

Serves 6

600g trout fillets
10g freshly ground pepper
16g salt
4 egg whites
½ litre Crème Fraiche

Mix the fish, salt and pepper; add the egg whites and once the mixture has become even and smooth, add the cream.

Butter a cake mould or the ring shaped Charlotte mould and half fill with the mousse

Place the mould into the oven in a 'bain-marie' with pre-heated water. Leave in the oven for about 45 minutes.

This dish can be eaten hot or cold and can be frozen easily but be aware it takes a quite a while to defrost.

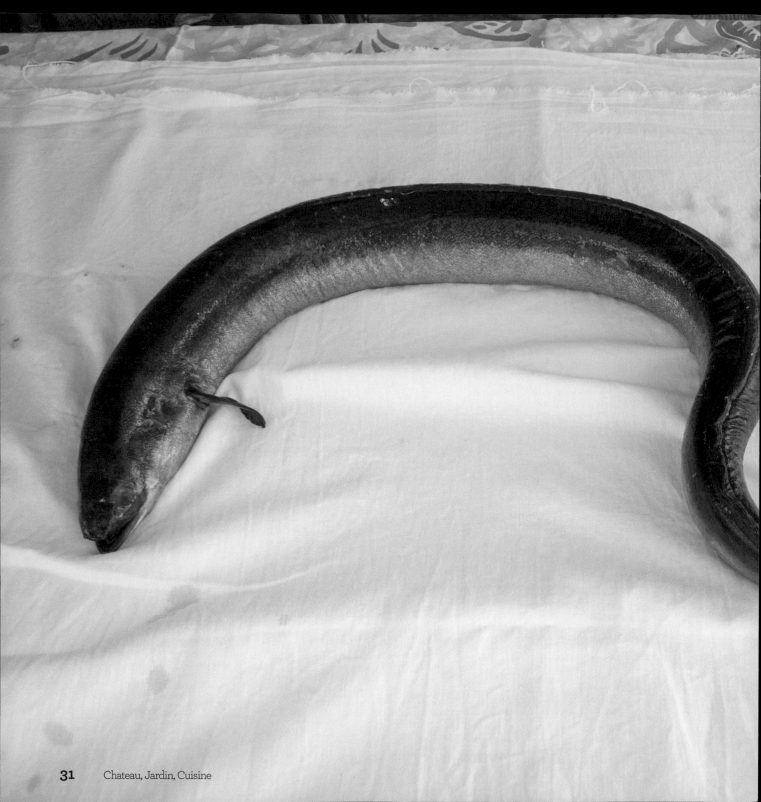

Eels in the Ardèche Region

t is a fact that global developments often are mirrored in the seemingly remote and secluded region of the Ardèche. Such is the story of the eel. Once the rivers and ponds were teeming with this fish and it was a staple food: cheap, nutritious and readily available. Eels were renowned for their robustness, which was also due to their ability to breathe air and to overcome obstacles by going through moist meadows or climb up the mossy walls of weirs. The wet zones or corridors that made their migration possible, hardly exist anymore and have been built over; obstacles such as fishways and dams have increased in numbers and size. In addition, turbines are more common and are dangerous to large fish. However, what truly has reduced the population of this fabled and mysterious fish is pollution. The eel is one of the greatest migrants. European eels grow up in the freshwater rivers and in estuaries of Europe. They then swim several thousand kilometres using the currents of the Atlantic until they reach the Sargasso Sea, a 2-million-square-mile warm water region in the North Atlantic, where they hatch. In their journey across the Atlantic, they go into very deep waters and very little is known about them during this period. It is believed that the pressure of the water is needed for ovulation to take place and it is known that the grown fish are extremely sensitive to light. They are nocturnal fish. Therefore, their downstream migration takes place at night. In the Sargasso, the larvae grow into translucent small eels of about 15 cm - the elvers - whose skin is very thin and delicate and could particularly sensitive to pollution: such as lead, other metals and the numerous agricultural pesticides. Afterwards, the young eels ride the ocean currents until they reach freshwater rivers anywhere from Greenland to South America or the Ardèche. It is very likely that the warming of the seas will affect them, as also the change of direction of water streams.

In the European estuaries, where their parents originated, the little eels by now about 30 cm, turn into young or yellow eels and start living at the bottom of the rivers, estuaries or ponds. It is here that pollution could be the most damaging factor. Depending on the temperature, they become sedentary and colonise the estuaries or swim upstream. The adult eels are silver skinned and live for at least 10 years, after that time they journey back over the Atlantic to the Sargasso, where they lay their eggs and die.

It is estimated that since the 1980-90, the eel population has been depleted by more than 90%. Since 2007, the European Union considers them a species threatened with extinction and has set up a restoration plan. Eels, particularly elvers, are considered a delicacy in Spain, in Japan and in many other cuisines, and now have become very expensive. Greenpeace has added eels to its Seafood Red List, which means that there is a high risk of their being sourced from unsustainable fisheries. In France, the government has regulated the fishing of eels and thus is helping to rebuild the eel population. It has also banned fishing from polluted rivers.

We would give eel a break for a while and recommend using a more sustainable replacement such as catfish for this great looking recipe. Catfish has been caught and consumed for centuries in North America, Africa, Asia, and Europe, and is much easier to farm-raise than eel.

7. Stewed Eel

This is a recipe from the era when fishing eels was very common. The traditional method was to stretch a rope across the river overnight, attach many baited lines and come back in the early morning to a very bountiful catch. Nowadays, fishing eels is strictly regulated and it is not easy to get a fishing permit. As a result the dishes have disappeared from the Ardèche cuisine. We don't want them to disappear from memory, however, and if you want to try this interesting dish, it is advisable to order your fish a week in advance with a fishmonger. We went to the Poissonnerie Griffone in Aubenas - without ordering - and luckily there was an eel on offer. Its weight was close to 2 kilograms. The classical Ardèche recipe is for younger and smaller eels and it is a case of simply frying them for 7 to 8 minutes with butter, parsley and garlic. The skin of eels is very tough and was formerly used for belts and drains. Nearly everyone remembers that the skin of eels has to be peeled from the head down. However, when we tried to do this with our big one, we found that it needed 2 strong men. Therefore, it is advisable to ask your fishmonger to skin and clean your fish. The meat, on the other hand, has a firmer consistency than that of younger eels.

1 big Eel, skinned, cleaned and cut into sections of about 2 to 3 cm
1 cup of chopped sorrel
1 cup of chopped spinach
1 cup of chopped parsley
1 cup of tarragon
1 sprig of sage
1 sprig of thyme
3 laurel leaves
2 cloves of garlic
Juice of half a lemon
1 glass of dry white wine
200ml single cream
2 egg yolks

Melt some butter in a large pan and sweat the sorrel, the spinach, the parsley, the tarragon and the sage. Then add the eel pieces and after a couple of minutes, thyme and laurel leaves. Simmer for approximately 10 minutes and towards the end, add the white wine. Simmer for another 3 to 4 minutes and pour in the lemon juice and the cream and, once you have removed it from the heat, stir in the egg yolks.

Traditionally this is served with a relatively dry white wine such as Chardonnay.

8. Caillettes

This is the essential Ardèche recipe, a kind of herby meatball. There are as many variations as there are cooks. Each winter, Mado and her husband prepare about 30 kilos of these delicious meatballs for the family and their friends. She makes them small, ideal for these aperitifs, which will last a whole summer evening and are most enjoyable where a great variety of starters are served. Caillettes are a natural part of every buffet or picnic. This recipe can be prepared in advance and Caillettes are very suitable for freezing.

Serves 6 to 10

2kg fresh Swiss chard or spinach leaves, in order to obtain 1 kilogram of cooked vegetables
1kg pork (half rib meat, half pork belly)
Salt: 10g per kilogram
Pepper and Thyme
Four Spice: Cinnamon, Cloves, Ginger & Nutmeg

Only use the green parts of the Kale or Swiss chard leaves and cook them in water for about 20 minutes. Take out and place on a dry towel. Put the leaves overnight in the refrigerator and weigh them down so that all water is pressed out. Mado recommends a stone, but remembers that in her childhood days a tractor wheel was used. The next day, pass the meat through a meat grinder and mix it together in a large bowl. Spread out and sprinkle with the Four Spice, thyme and salt and then give a few good turns with the pepper mill. Add the cooked and pressed kale and mix well using your hands. Make small meatballs, keeping them the same size. Place these close together in a well-greased, ovenproof dish. Traditionalists wrap them in pork Caul (a transparent membrane around the intestines of pigs and calves, also called Crow) so that they keep their shape and stay firmer. In this case, you should start by rinsing the Caul in a bit of water with vinegar. Place the Caillettes in the oven at 200°c for about 30 minutes.

Serve either cold or warm with a Cabernet Sauvignon wine.

9. Summer Salad

Serves 6:

1 big head of radicchio salad, about 600 grams
1 ripe mango
500g asparagus - only the halves with the heads
500g green beans
2 tbs Acacia honey
4 tbs Ricotta or fresh goats cheese

For the dressing:

2 tbs soya sauce
Juice of 1 small lemon
1 tsp Acacia honey
2 tbs Walnut oil
2 tbs Olive oil
Pepper

Wash the salads, cut the radicchio leaves to edible size. Steam the runner beans by pouring very little water into a pot, bring it to the boil and throw in the runner beans and cook for 7 minutes. Do the same with the asparagus.

Our wine suggestion: serve with a Beaujolais Blanc.

10. Terrine of Pork and Duck

This homemade terrine is delicious and easy to make. Ask your butcher to mince the meat for you. Rabbit or veal may be used instead of pork. For the liver, one should count 1 kilo of liver for 1 kilo of meat. Unless, you are as lucky as Marlo and someone gives you the liver of a wild boar. In this case, reduce the amount of liver since it tastes stronger and could overwhelm the terrine.

400g liver of pork or wild boar
400g pork and duck fillet (with skin)
200g streaky bacon
12g salt
2 tbs Armagnac
Pepper, thyme, rosemary, bay leaf powder

Cut the meats, the bacon and the liver in pieces, then mince it all in a mixer. Place it in a large bowl and mix with the spices and the Armagnac. Put into an ovenproof dish, preferably an oval dish for terrines and cover it with the skin from the duck's breast. Add a few sprigs of thyme. Cover with a lid and cook in the oven at 200° for an hour to 1½ hours depending on the quantity. It is done when a knife comes out clean when you make a cut. Leave to cool for at least 3 hours. Decorate with gherkins and radishes or red peppercorns and serve the terrine in big slices on a salad leaf.

11. Chicken Liver Soufflé

Serves 6

This wonderful and light soufflé becomes a complete meal when it is served with Quenelles 'Nature'. The latter are a speciality from around Lyon and have found popularity in the Ardèche. You can buy them easily, but make sure that they are not in a tin. For the soufflé, we used chicken livers, but rabbit livers make an equally delicious dish. They are much smaller and a rabbit liver soufflés is a hot starter rather than a main course.

500g mushrooms
200g black olives
1 large onion
4 cloves of garlic (medium)
½ baguette (dry)
6 eggs
3 tbs parsley, chopped
4 chicken livers

Start by soaking the dry bread in milk. Season the tomato coulis, add the mushrooms and olives, then cook these gently over a low heat. During this time, put the onion, the garlic, the bread, the chopped parsley and the livers into a blender and mix them together.

For the soufflé: Preheat the oven to 200° to 210°. While it heats up, prepare a thick béchamel sauce. Take it off the heat and add the onion-liver mixture as well as the egg yolks and season with salt and pepper. Then whip the egg whites until they are very firm and gently fold them into the béchamel and liver mixture. Put it into small porcelain soufflé dishes that are buttered and powdered with flour. Make them about half full and then bake in the oven for 40 minutes. Test whether they are done by piercing the centre with the tip of a sharp knife. The knife has to come out clean.

For the accompaniment: 3/4 litre tomato coulis (see recipe below) and 6 quenelles nature, if you choose to. Since the quenelles will expand, it is best to place them in the coulis about 40 minutes before you plan to serve the dish and leave them to cook gently.

12. Tomato Coulis

The ideal time to make tomato coulis is in September when the tomatoes have soaked up the sun of the summer. If you use fresh tomatoes from the garden they could provide you with a coulis that is much better than anything you buy and which can last for the rest of the year.

For 1½ litres of coulis

3kg fresh tomatoes or tinned tomatoes
2 large onions,
3 cloves of garlic
Salt and pepper
5 sprigs of parsley, basil or thyme

Wash the tomatoes and peel them using boiling water. Should you need to save time, you can also press the finished sauce through a sieve in order to remove the pips and the skin.

Sweat the onions and the garlic in olive oil and add the tomatoes, cut into pieces. Season the mixture with salt and pepper. For the recipe of the chicken liver soufflé, you should add the parsley. For other recipes either basil or thyme may be used. Let the sauce simmer gently for 45 minutes. Mix it well before putting it into plastic boxes or freezer bags.

A traditional suggestion to preserve the coulis, is to pour it hot into sterilised jars that close hermetically and to add some oil on top before closing the jars and storing them in a dry place away from sunlight. However, from a professional point of view, to gain an unlimited shelf life, the coulis would need to be hot packed into sterilised containers with a pH of less than 4.5.

For practical reasons, our suggestion for conservation is to pour the coulis - once it has cooled off - into plastic boxes or freezer bags, in order to save space, and simply to deep freeze it.

13. Red Pepper Tarte

n Spring, peppers are plentiful. This vegetarian tart embodies the freshness of Spring. It is also rather quickly produced, even when you make the shortcrust pastry yourself, which will taste much better, of course. This delicious tart can also be served in small bites as an aperitif.

Serves 4

For the shortcrust pastry:
250g flour
125g butter
½ glass of cold water
1 pinch of fine salt

For the filling - a purée of peppers:
5 red peppers
2 onions
1 clove of garlic
1 Bouquet Garni (bay leaves, thyme, parsley), salt and pepper

Sift the flour into a large bowl and add the softened butter in small pieces together with the salt. Mix with your fingers until the mixture resembles grains of couscous. Add just about half a glass of cold water into a hollow you make in the centre and mix it without kneading it too much. Then roll it into a ball and leave it for at least 1 hour. This pastry can easily be kept in the deep freezer.

Chop the onions and sweat them quickly over high heat together with the garlic, the herbs, pepper, salt and the peppers in a big frying pan or a wok and let cook over low heat for ¾ hours stirring the mixture from time to time.

Spread the pastry over a pie plate. Spread the pepper mixture over the pastry. Cook in the oven at 180° for 20 to 30 minutes.

14. Homemade Bread

Mado and her sister Simone make their bread in the beautiful Mas de L'Abeille. This ancient sheep and silk farm is hidden in the rocky land near the village of Labeaume. Since the 60s it has been lovingly restored by the Petits Chanteurs de St.Louis, a charity for children. You'll find several kitchens and rooms with huge fireplaces, but the best is the bread oven in one of the courtyards.

Mado and Simone begin in the early morning with a good fire, so that the bed of hot ashes is just ready when the dough is prepared. Many people will stop by, since the sisters are well known for their skills, and all of them depart happily with a loaf of warm bread.

1 kg flour
30g yeast for bread (or Alsacienne yeast)
600g water
30g salt
2 egg yolks
60g butter

This recipe can be made with most kind of flours. Make the dough by kneading in a large bowl and leave it to rise for at least 2 hours covered lightly with a cotton sheet. Once the dough is about twice the original volume, deflate it by working it with your hands. Sprinkle a bit of flour on a tray and shape the dough in not too large balls or sticks or rings. Cover it and, again, leave let it inflate. In a bowl, mix 1 egg yolk, a pinch of salt and a teaspoon of warm water and paste onto the balls, sticks and rings. Leave them to rest in a warm room for ¼ hour.

If you have a bread oven: extinguish the flames and work on the ashes. Push the remaining wood to the back of the oven and sprinkle a bit of flour in order to test the temperature. Should it turn dark or black, the oven is still too hot. Once the temperature is right, place the bread inside the oven and bake for about ½ hour – depending on the size.

If you use your normal oven, place a bowl of water with your bread. Since bread is traditionally baked in a cooling oven, start with 220° for 10 minutes, to give it that boost

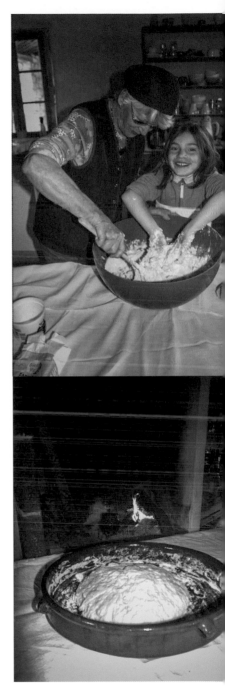

and kill off the yeast, then turn it down to 180° for the rest of the time, which is another 35 minutes for a small loaf. The size of loaves and to an extent, what they have in them affects the timing. You do want it properly cooked right through to the middle. .

For bread with nuts the rules are simple: prepare 1 kg of dough and leave to rise for 1 hour. Add 150 grams of nut kernels, chopped roughly, and continue with the recipe. You need to paste it with 2 egg yolks and 60 grams of butter and set it aside for 1 hour before it goes into the oven for 45 minutes.

15. Soufflé of Goats Cheese

This delicate soufflé is made with fresh goats cheese or 'Faisselle', which is similar to a fromage blanc, but gives a more refined flavour. To make this starter even more interesting, mix some fresh chives, chopped finely, into the cheese mixture.

Serves 4

3 egg yolks
5 egg whites
250g fresh goat's cheese or 'Faisselle' (at 20% fat)
1 tbs olive oil
Salt, pepper and nutmeg
Grated Parmesan for decoration

Preheat the oven to 180° C. In a bowl, first mix the yolks and then add the goats' cheese and the olive oil. Season with salt, pepper and ground nutmeg and mix well. Beat the whites with a pinch of salt until they are really firm. Fold them gently into the egg and cheese mixture together with the chives. Fill this into small ovenproof dishes, which you have buttered lightly.

Cook in the oven for 12 minutes. Take out, decorate with the grated Parmesan and red peppercorns and serve immediately.

16. Savoury Cake with Courgettes

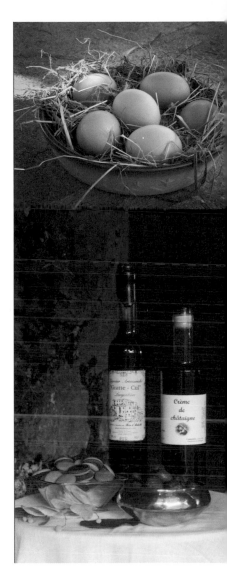

This is a recipe from the South Ardèche. It can be served hot or cold, but preferably warm and if combined with an interesting salad, you have a simple but complete meal. Also, cut it into small pieces and it will be a winner at picnics and aperitifs.

Serves 6 to 8

For the pastry:

500g flour
1 packet of yeast
250g butter
250g water
1 tsp salt

Sieve the flour into a roomy bowl and mix it with the yeast as well as the salt. Make a hole in the middle.

Heat the butter gently in a small pot. Once completely melted, add the same volume of cold water and pour this mixture into the hole you made in the flour. Mix with a wooden spoon until you obtain a ball. Leave to rest for at least 1 hour. During this time prepare the topping.

For the garnish of courgettes:

1 kg courgettes (organic)
200g Gruyere cheese (grated)
2 eggs
Salt, Pepper and 1 tsp Cumin

Steam the courgettes whole with their skin and stalks. Once they are soft, gently press out their water with your hands. Squash them with a fork or, if you prefer, a mixer if you prefer. Add the grated cheese and the spices. Whisk the eggs and add them as well. This will give you a purée, which will go into your pastry.

Preparation of the pastry:

Prepare an egg yolk for the golden look. Preferably use a square cake tin of about 40cm x 25cm, since you want to use every bit of the cake after you cut it up. Also, it is preferable to use a stainless steel rolling pin. It will make the job easier. Beat the pastry a couple of times; this will make it fluffier later. Once the pastry is ready to be rolled out, separate the ball into 2 halves for the base and the cover. Place a rolled out layer at the bottom of the cake tin and fill It with the courgette mixture and then cover it with the 2nd half of rolled out pastry. Close the pastry ends well by using a bit of water. With a brush, paint it with the egg yolk.

Place the cake in the oven at 180° for about 30 minutes, but keep an eye on it.

17. La Croustade

This recipe is about using thrushes and you will hopefully make allowances for the lack of political correctness. This book is as much about the traditions that have fed into Ardèche cuisine as it is about our modern ways of using the typical products of this region.

The recipe comes from the extreme South of the Vivarais where people live as they do in Provence. Thrushes are plentiful here in winter, when they come down from the Ardèche Mountains in search of the last forgotten grapes or juniper and laurel berries. These birds are a delicacy and they are eagerly awaited during the shooting season. Before cooking them, one should hang them in a cool and dry place for six to eight days, depending on how much one likes the taste of game. There is no need to gut them. For our recipe, we were given 8 thrushes, which is enough to make an excellent starter for 4 people.

Roll the birds into rashers of not too salty bacon. Then make little parcels with string. Cook them gently in butter for about ½ hour. Take the parcels apart and take the bones out with a small, sharp knife and throw them away. Keep the bacon, cut it into small pieces, and put it together with the meat. Add 1 to 2 tbsp of mustard to the meat as well as a glass of white wine and mix well. This mixture is already your Croustade.

Preheat the oven to 200°. Fill the Croustade into small ramekins or into a large one and cook in the oven for about ½ hour. Place a baking tray of small bread slices in the same oven. However, you have to check them regularly while the Croustade is baking. Serve on a bed of mixed leaves, decorated   if you happen to be in range - with 'Mélange Salade', sold by Ghyslaine on her wonderful herb stall at the markets of Largentière, Joyeuse, Ruoms and Les Vans.

18. Savoury Carrot Cake

This soft cake gets an exotic flavour from the cumin and sweetness from the raisins. When you are inviting friends to drinks that are a bit more substantial and where people just stay on, this is a very interesting addition.

Serves 6

500g grated carrots
2 onions
1 clove of garlic
4 eggs
1 tbs cumin powder
125g ground hazelnuts
1 handful dried raisins
2 tbs olive oil
1 tbs flour
2 tbs hazelnut oil
Salt, pepper, chilli powder

Grate the carrots; slice the onion finely and sweat it in olive oil so that it gets slightly caramelised. Chop or press the garlic and mix all the ingredients together in a bowl. Then season with salt, pepper and a knife tip of chilli powder.

Preheat the oven to 210°.

Pour the mixture into a cake mould and bake in the oven 35 to 40 minutes.
Serve with a few gherkins and some radishes.

19. Pumpkin and Chestnut Cream

During the surprising and sudden chilliness of October and November, there is nothing better than a good soup. This autumn cream will be even more delicious if you use homemade chicken stock. Should you not have fresh or good dried chestnuts, it is possible to use chestnut purée, which is much easier to find outside the Ardèche and out of season. For a more sophisticated meal, you might want to serve this soup in espresso cups with tiny bits of dried chestnut.

Serves 6 to 8

1.5 kg pumpkin peeled
2cm ginger root peeled and grated
1 knob of butter
1 carrot
1 mild onion
350g chestnuts
2 pistils of saffron
4-5 cardamoms
1 pinch of cinnamon
1 clove of garlic in its skin
1L chicken stock, homemade, or vegetable stock for vegetarians
Salt, pepper according to taste
Crème fraîche, according to taste

Place the saffron into a bit of hot water for about 20 minutes, to be used with the crème fraiche later. Cut the onion into slices and in a frying pan sweat in a bit of butter until golden. Add the spices and fry for a couple of seconds each. Then add the whole garlic clove with its skin, the carrot and the pumpkin cut into small pieces. Pour in the stock and the chestnuts chopped into small bits. Save a few to garnish the soup. Bring to the boil and gently cook for 30 minutes. At the end, take out the garlic clove, and mix the soup. Add the crème fraîche, into which you have mixed the safran, and add salt and pepper according to taste.

Garnish the soup with small pieces of chestnut and flat parsley or coriander.

20. Chicken Stock

This homemade stock has a delicate and refined flavour. It is easy to make but one should only use the highest quality of ingredients. We buy free range chicken and since we live fairly close to the farm of Serge et Christine Tachon, we can confirm that their chickens seem to have a good life. Up to a certain point.

For 1 litre of stock:

The bones or carcass of 1 chicken carcass; or
1kg chicken wings, which are easy and cheap to buy
2 carrots
1 or 2 leeks, the white part only, but keep the green leaves for another good soup
1 big onion into which you stick a clove
1 bay leaf, a sprig of thyme, a stalk of parsley
Salt and pepper

Place the meat with the onion and the herbs in a pan or in a pressure cooker and cover them with at least 1 ½ litres of water. Bring to the boil and skim off the foam that will appear. Then, add the washed and peeled vegetables, cover the pan with a lid and leave to simmer for at least 2 hours or 1 hour in the pressure cooker. Salt and pepper can be added at the very end or even when you use the stock in other recipes.

Pour the soup through a fine strainer and only keep the liquid, which you leave to cool completely. Don't forget to skim away the layer of fat that forms on the stock once it is cold.

You can frieze the stock in small containers or freezer bags and use it as needed: for a bouillon with vermicelles and/or raw and thinly sliced vegetables, soya sauce, or ginger and herbs such as coriander and chervil. Another good idea is to poach an egg in this chicken stock together with finely chopped parsley and a bit of lemon juice. This stock can also be used as the basis for soups with chestnuts, carrots, split peas or for a good onion soup.

21. Cream of Nettle Soup

Nettles only grow on damp and healthy soil. They appear in spring and it is easy to pick them on the banks of the Labaume River. Nettles can produce a powerful fertilizer once fermented and some farmers still know how to dilute this, use it and live with the smell.

The nettle is also known for its medicinal qualities. It can be drunk as a diuretic tea; it is used in pomades against problems with hair and it is also said to help with rheumatism. Nettles are rich in proteins, in vitamins A and C, in calcium and iron and also in potassium and magnesium. However, we are mainly interested in the nettle's culinary qualities. For this delicious and interesting soup, you need to start by picking a handful of young nettle leaves.

Cooking time 45 minutes.

Serves 6

300g young nettle leaves
1 Leek
4 medium sized potatoes
2.5L salted water or chicken stock
4 carrots
300ml Crème Fraîche
Pepper, nutmeg

Peel the potatoes and cut them into small cubes. Clean the leek and cut leek and carrots into small slices. Cook the leek, carrots, potatoes and the nutmeg in 1½ litres of salted water or chicken stock. Leave to boil gently for 25 minutes. During this time, take the nettle leaves off the stems and rinse them in water. Towards the end, add the leaves into the leek, carrot, potato mixture and leave to simmer for another 5 to 10 minutes. Mix well with a good mixer. Add the crème fraîche and pepper and serve immediately.

22. La Cousina or Cream of Chestnut Soup

The chestnut is the signature product of the Ardèche. In the past, it gave the land its soul and character and there is a revival today with the creation of les Mons de l'Ardèche, a national park dedicated to the preservation of the tree. We, still, have some very interesting recipes such as this simple chestnut soup called La Cousina. It has become a classical dish renowned beyond the county. It has a delicate flavour and can be a heartening and warming lunch especially when served with a glass of white wine.

Serves 4 to 6

500g chestnuts completely peeled. Keep a couple for decoration.
½L salted water
½L milk
3-4 tbsp Crème Fraiche
1 Celery stick or celery salt
Salt, Pepper

Preparation: Cook the chestnuts in water once you have peeled off the hard skin with the help of a small very sharp knife. Once they are cooked, take them out of the water with a skimmer and take off the second skin. This has to be done while they are hot. It is much easier with a variety of chestnuts that has fewer divisions so that tno bits of skin will be left in the fruit.

The soup: Bring the salted water or bouillon and the milk to the boil and then add the peeled chestnuts with the nutmeg. Leave to simmer for at least 1 hour. Towards the end, add the celery stick or the celery salt. Then mix the soup and season with salt and pepper. Add 2 to 4 tablespoons of crème fraiche according to taste and leave to simmer for a little longer. If the soup gets too thick, add a mixture of milk and water. Leave to rest and cool off. Decorate with the broken chestnut pieces and serve.

23. Cream of Porcini

Once autumn has arrived and the days are misty, there is one kind of mushroom that everyone wants to find in the woods: the porcini. They are at their best when they still have their corklike shape and when eaten fresh. You can, however, dry them and thus enjoy them all year long. The secret of this simple soup, which is full of flavours, is to use a generous amount of porcini.

Serves 4 to 6

500g Porcini
3 cloves of garlic
2L chicken stock
2 tbs parsley
12-20dl Crème Fraîche

Clean the porcini without washing them and cut them in small pieces. If you are using dried mushrooms, soak them in hot water. Brown the porcini in a bit of olive oil for a maximum of 1 minute. Bring the bouillon to boiling point in a saucepan. Cut and mix garlic and parsley roughly and add the mix to the mushrooms and brown a bit longer. Add a good ladle of the bouillon to the mushrooms and then pour them into the bouillon. Leave to cook for 15 minutes in order to reduce the liquid. Mix the soup and add pepper according to taste. Take off the heat and add the crème fraîche.

Decorate with parsley and serve.

24. Aubergines à la Provencale

Vegetarian dishes are still a rarity in the traditional Ardèche cuisine and we had to look hard and invent a few recipes to be up to date. Use ripe and firm aubergines for this refreshing dish, which is a great favourite during the summer months.

Serves 3 to 4

4 aubergines
1 bunch of parsley
1 clove of garlic
½L tomato coulis (see page 46)

Peel the aubergines and cut them in slices of less than a centimetre. Cut a grid into each slice and rub them with salt. Leave to rest for 2 hours in a strainer. They will give out quite a bit of water. Later rinse the aubergine slices and dry them on a clean towel. Fry them gently in very hot vegetable oil until both sides are golden brown. Once the frying is done, leave them on kitchen towels so that the oil gets absorbed. Place the aubergines on a plate; pour a thin line of olive oil over them. Then sprinkle with the garlic cut in tiny pieces and pour the hot coulis over the aubergines. At the very end, sprinkle generously with finely cut parsley.

1Kg

Produit

soit le kg ___ €

12 90€

Chanterelle

Variété

Catégorie   Calibre

Origine

II

550

25. Spinach and Goat Cheese Pies

This traditional French pie is a dish of meat or vegetables cooked wrapped in pastry. This nourishing recipe is a full meal and luckily there is more to life than pasta and mash for our vegetarian teenagers.

The pastry called Pâte Brisée is the French version of the classic pie or tart pastry, also often called short crust pastry. It is very versatile and is used for sweet and savory pies and you can even frieze it.

Preparation: 45 min; cooking time 35 min.

For 6 small pies: one per person

For the pastry:
250g flour
125g butter, cut into small cubes
50ml water
1 egg yolk
1 level tsp salt

For the filling:
3 fresh goat's cheeses
350g button mushrooms, cleaned and chopped
400g spinach, stalks removed
1 small onion, finely sliced
2 garlic cloves, pressed
1 egg
2 tbs thick Crème Fraiche
3 tbs olive oil
Salt, pepper, nutmeg

Utensils:
6 small round pastry or muffin moulds 7.5 cm in diameter and 4 cm high

To make the pastry, dilute the salt in the water; pour the flour into a bowl and make a hole in the centre. Add the butter, the salted water and the egg yolk. Gently mix the ingredients, adding a bit of water if necessary. Knead the mixture swiftly and then wrap it in cling film. If you form a round disc rather than a ball, it will refrigerate more quickly and be easier to roll out. Leave to rest for half an hour.

Lightly brown the onion in a frying pan with the olive oil. Add the sliced mushrooms and season with salt and pepper. Cook the mixture until the water of the mushrooms has evaporated. Once the mushrooms start to get a golden colour, add the chopped spinach. Continue to cook for about 2 minutes – just long enough to get the leaves to wilt. Take off the heat and add the pressed garlic and some grated nutmeg. Pour the mixture into a bowl. Add the cheeses cut into small pieces, the egg and the crème fraiche.

Spread the pastry out on a board sprinkled with flour until it is about 1.5 mm thick. Cut out 6 circles of 13.5 cm in diameter and 6 circles of 7 cm. Cover your buttered and floured moulds with the big circles of pastry. Fill them with the spinach-cheese mixture and lightly press down with the back of a spoon. Fold over the border of the pastry and baste with the egg yolk. Then stick a small pastry disk on top so that the spinach mixture is completely enveloped. Again baste the top with egg yolk and place the pies in the oven for about 35 min at 180°. They are ready when the pastry has a golden colour.

Take out of the moulds and serve hot with a good mixed salad.

26. La Bombine

There is much more to the Ardèche's cuisine than chestnuts, although its classic dishes are by no means cutting edge. Most have a rustic, country taste that reflects the region's self-sufficiency. Pâtés and hams are excellent, as are the creamy goat's cheeses, the most famous of which is the Picodon. A special place is reserved for the Bombine, a garlicky potato gratin served as an accompaniment to red wine-based stews with pork or goat meat. For dessert, much use is made of chestnuts again, but also of summer fruits, like billberries and raspberries that grow copiously throughout the countryside.

The Bombine used to be called the 'Dish of the Poor' because it is a complete meal with potatoes and a little meat. Bay leaves give this dish a special aroma, but otherwise the ingredients can vary widely and there are as many recipes for Bombine as there are villages in the Ardèche. Saint Andéol de Berg is called the Capital of the Bombine with chefs called Maîtres Bombinaires. Some of them will add carrots, garlic or black olives. Here we offer you a recipe from the beautiful village of Labeaume, which is home of Mado and her family.

Serves 6

1.5kg potatoes
2 onions
4 bay leaves
2 sprigs of thyme
1 Glass of white wine
800gram salted pork belly or smoked bacon
Pepper

Peel the potatoes and cut them into not too small cubes. Cut the meat into smaller pieces and slice the onions finely. Pour a bit of olive oil into a cast iron casserole dish and sweat the onions and brown the meat. Then moisten both with half a litre of salted water and the white wine. Throw in thyme and bay leaves and pepper and bring to boiling point. Then, add the potatoes and cover with the lid and place in the oven at medium temperature for 1½ to 2 hours. Serve the bombine with a crisp salad for a simple but exquisite meal.

27. Fillet of Beef 'Fin Gras'

On the mountain region of Mézenc, which is in both the Haute-Loire and the Ardèche, there is a tradition of fattening cattle, which results in a meat called Fin Gras du Mézenc. Over the winter months, young animals are fed exclusively on hay perfumed with local herbs and flowers, in particular the Meum athamanticum, a plant in the Apiaceae family, commonly called Spignel and Meu. The meat is studded with intramuscular fat, similar to Kobe beef, and its taste is so particular and fine that it has been granted the prestigious Appellation d'Origine Contrôlée (AOC). Usually, it is hung for about 10 days and comes to the market around Easter time. For this reason it is also called 'Boeuf de Pacques'.

Serves 6

900g to 1kg beef fillet 'Fin Gras de Mézenc'
1 bunch radishes
1 bunch baby asparagus
1 long turnip
½ litre chicken stock

Cut the turnip and the radishes in fine slices, but leave the asparagus whole. Cook the asparagus separately from the turnip, each in half the chicken stock, but leave the radishes uncooked.

Roasting the meat: preheat the oven to 220°, then lower to 200° and cook for a maximum of 20 minutes. This meat is served pink. Decorate with the vegetables sprinkled with lemon juice. Their three colours will be a wonderful contrast to the meat and will bring the Spring to your table.

28. Fillet of Duck and Glazed Chestnuts

The Tajine is the quintessential Moroccan dish. Its name alone evokes the scents of the Maghreb and visions of dishes cooked slowly over charcoal fire. This recipe, however, is made with ingredients from the Ardèche and only uses the Tajine cooking method.

The most difficult part could be sourcing the 'marrons confits' or glazed chestnuts if you are not in the Ardèche. Better to order them online from Clément Faugier http://www.clementfaugier.fr or from Maison Imbert www.marrons-imbert.com. In Largentière, in a former Magnanerie, a large house where silkworms used to be grown, is L'Ardéchoise (www.lardechoise.net), one of the best shops to buy truly local chestnut products. The enthusiastic and sympathetic owner Frédéric Lavesque will show you his chestnut sorting machine and will let you try his crème de marrons, which is made with less sugar and no vanilla, because according to him chestnuts from the Ardèche do not need such additives to enhance their taste. The only chestnut product you won't be able to buy at L'Ardéchoise are Marrons Glacés because this delicacy is made with Italian chestnuts, the Marrons de Naples, who do not go soft when cooked in sugar but keep their texture underneath a crispy icing.

Serves 6

2 duck fillets (with skin)
2 tbs olive oil or vegetable oil
2 pinches of ground coriander
1 tin of 500 grams of glazed (confit) chestnuts
1 tsp lemon juice
1 chicken stock (half a cube in a big glass of boiling water)

Rub the meat with the coriander, then with oil, salt and pepper. Brown it in a frying pan in

butter and oil. Lightly coat it with some of the syrup of the chestnuts. You could add some chestnuts to the syrup in order to thicken the sauce.

Place it in the oven in an ovenproof dish for 20 minutes. Do not forget to baste the fillets with the chicken stock. The fillets are normally eaten rare or pink, but they can sit and wait for a little while. Towards the end, add chestnuts according to your taste, but count at least two per person. Dribble some lemon juice over the meat.

While the meat is in the oven, prepare some seasonal vegetables to accompany the meat, such as carrots, turnips, spring onions, Brussels sprouts, pumpkin, garlic. Cut the vegetables into smallish cubes and brown them in butter in a Tajine dish. Afterwards pour in the chicken or vegetable stock, add a branch of thyme and cover with a lid. Cook for about 30 minutes. If you wish, you could add some small boiled potatoes in the last 10 minutes. Serve together with the meat in the Tajine dish.

An alternative way of making this dish is to add the chestnuts to the vegetables rather than to the meat. Or, you could replace the duck with pork filet or leg of lamb. In the latter scenario, it is important to coat it with a white wine-bouillon-thyme mixture.

29. Black Pudding

Sausage making is an annual ritual and a family event. It was part of 'La Tuade', a day during the cold months of November and December, when pigs used to be slaughtered on the farms. Neighbouring families took it in turn to organise this important event. The pigs used to be reared by the farmers themselves and literally every part of the animal was used and converted into sausages, meatballs, ham and other delicacies. At the end of this big day, the freshly made black pudding sausages are served with apples fried in butter as a reward for everyone.

However, due to the Health and Safety regulations, this cultural practice has become an extremely rare event even in rural Ardèche. Very few people now have the opportunity of slaughtering their own pig. However, it is still worthwhile just making the black pudding. Ask your butcher or a wholesaler to reserve some blood and guts for this. Guts can even come from China nowadays and then they might be artificial and people refer to them as 'Chinois'. The natural guts should be rinsed two or three times. However, should you buy them in a big supermarket, they would be preserved in salt and you need to rinse them 5 or 6 times with warm and clean water and then one last time with cold water. Make sure that you have a few helpers since the filling of the sausages into the slippery guts would be hard to manage on your own. At Mado's house, there is a strict division of labour: her husband makes a fire in the courtyard and heats water in a huge cauldron to the required 90°. Once it is steaming over the lively fire, the sausages should be ready and will be carefully lowered into the water. From time to time they are lifted out to check. One cannot help thinking of *'Double, double, toil and trouble. Fire burn and cauldron bubble...'*

Serves 10

3L pig's blood
1L Crème Fraiche
1L milk
1 stale white bread
200ml orange flower aroma
800g spinach, chopped
1kg onions
1 tbs olive oil
Salt, pepper, thyme or Four Spice (pepper, cloves, nutmeg and ginger)
5m guts for sausages (½ packet)

Soak the dry bread in the milk. Slice the onions and sweat them in a frying pan with butter. Add to the bread and mix well. Add the chopped spinach, mix well and then add the blood. Into this mixture, pour the orange aroma and the crème fraiche. Stir well and add the olive oil, salt, pepper, thyme or Four Spice.

Filling the guts: place a piece of gut of about 2 meters onto a funnel. Don't forget to make a knot at the other end. With a soup ladle transfer the blood mixture into the piece of gut. At this point, you could add some small pieces of lard. Close the gut with some fine string and repeat the procedure. The black pudding only will be cut into smaller sausages once it is cooked.

The next step is to make several bundles of the sausages that are not too heavy. Knot them tightly together and fold over a string and lower them into the water. It should be at 90 °. Add cold water if it is boiling. The sausages must not touch the walls of the pot, lest they burst. From time to time prick them with a long needle. They will be ready when they do not bleed. This will take about 11 minutes with natural gut, and about 15 minutes with the artificial 'Chinois'. Take the bundles out of the water and cover them with a towel because they need to continue to cook for a little while. Hang them for drying.

Peel and slice a few apples and fry the slices in butter. Cut the sausage into small pieces, quickly heat them up in the same frying pan and continue over low heat until crispy on the outside. Serve them on the apple slices.

30. Chicken Wings and Glazed Chestnuts

Wings are the tastiest part of the chicken and their meat is even more delicious if you go for a good corn fed chicken that has lived in some sort of freedom. Chicken wings are not costly and this dish – cooked with the Tajine method – is well worth the extra effort of dissecting it with your fingers. Place bowls with warm water on your table.

Serves 4

3 onions (if possible mild ones from the Cévennes)
1 or 2 carrots cut in big pieces
2 cloves of garlic
2 tbsp of vegetable oil and 1 tbsp of olive oil
12 chicken wings (top of wing)
1 cube of chicken stock in a large glass of boiling water
1 tsp of lemon juice
1 tsp ground cinnamon
1 tsp ground cumin
1 tsp ground coriander
12 glazed chestnuts in their syrup

Rub the chicken wings with a mixture of olive oil and the spices and fry them briefly in the vegetable oil together with the chopped onions. Later add the carrots and the garlic as well as salt and pepper. Sprinkle the meat with 3 to 4 tablespoons of the chestnut syrup and cook it either in the frying pan or at low heat (150°) in the oven for approximately 1½ hours. Keep an eye on it and add more liquid if necessary. Add the chestnuts towards the end of the cooking time. This dish can be prepared in advance and can be reheated.

An excellent side dish would be a purée of pumpkin and carrots cooked in vegetable stock and sprinkled with a bit of olive oil.

You can make a similar dish with mutton (shoulder cut into large pieces) or lamb (collar).

31. Potatoes Salad with Caillettes

This is a nourishing recipe and can be served as a single dish.

Serves 6

6 - 7 medium size potatoes
1 glass of white wine or chicken stock
2 Caillettes (see page 36)
1 – 2 onions, cut into fine slices

Peel the potatoes and cook them in salted water for about 20 minutes so that they stay firm. Do not let them become soft. Cut into chunky wedges or cubes and arrange the pieces in a deep serving platter or dish. Sprinkle wine or stock onto the potatoes so that they don't get dry and cover them with the onion slices. Season the potato dish with a vinaigrette of your choice, using olive oil or, vegetable oil or, if you have it, with a bit of walnut oil. On top put a layer of the crumbled Caillettes and serve with a crisp green salad.

32. Ossobuco with Lemon and Olives

The knuckle of veal or veal shanks or marrow bone is often better known as Ossobuco. It is nourishing and tastes great and we'll cook it with preserved lemon and some Harissa spice.

Serves 6

1.5kg or 2 to 3 tranches of Ossobuco
1 whole preserved lemon
1 onion, medium size
1 carrot
1 small branch of rosemary
200g green and black olives
80ml olive oil
2 tbs brown sugar
½ tsp harissa powder

Peel and cut onion and carrot into small pieces.

In a very hot casserole, or large pan, brown the tranches of Ossobuco for about 5 minutes on each side. Sprinkle with salt and pepper and continue until light brown. Lower the heat and add the onion and carrot. Cook them for 5 minutes and then add the lemon, cut in half, and the rosemary. Pour 600 ml of water into the casserole and add the sugar cubes and the Harissa. Cover with a lid and leave to simmer for 1½ hours turning the meat regularly.

After this, add the olives and continue to cook for another 30 minutes. Check whether the meat is cooked through and, if needed, add a bit of salt and pepper. Should the gravy be too watery, remove the meat and reduce the sauce.

Serve either with ratatouille or with courgettes sautéed with caraway seed powder.

33. Cottage Pie with Sweet Potatoes

Preparation time 20 minutes, cooking time 1 hour

Serves 6

4 duck thighs
300g sweet potatoes
300g potatoes
1 Fennel
3 sprigs parsley
1 onion
2 cloves garlic
1 glass milk
2 tbs cream
25g butter
Breadcrumbs

Season the duck thighs with salt and pepper and bake in a medium hot oven for 30 min. Once cooked, cut the meat off the bone and chop into small pieces. While the duck is cooking, make a purée with the sweet potato and the ordinary potatoes, the milk, the butter and the cream. Season with salt, pepper and 2 knife tips of chilli powder.

Cut the onion into fine slices and brown them in a bit of oil; add the chopped fennel and the parsley and cook for about half an hour until you have a compote.

In a buttered gratin dish place first a layer of the purée, then the duck pieces with a bit of their juice and then the fennel mixture and a last layer of potato purée. Sprinkle with breadcrumbs and place in the oven for 20 minutes at 180°.

Serve this dish very hot with a good green salad.

Suggestion: you can also use a Duck Confit without its fat, but be careful with the seasoning.

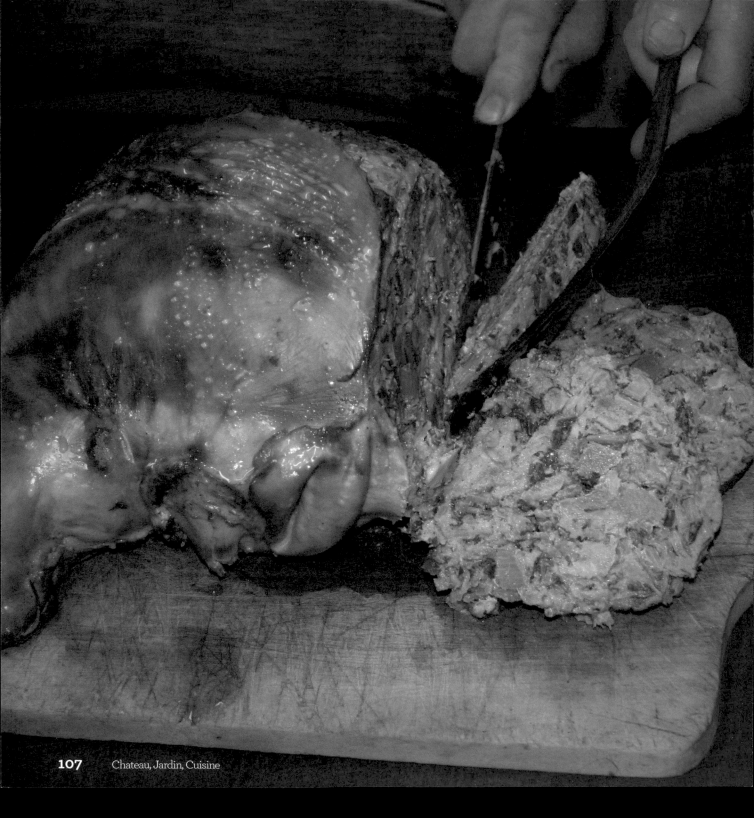

34. La Pouytrole

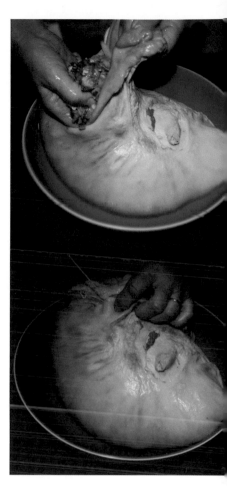

This famous dish is called Maouche on the Plateau in the North and Pouytrole in the South of the Ardéche. It consists of minced pork, prunes and cabbage cooked in a pig's stomach. In the South, spinach or Swiss chard replace the prunes and cabbage. La Maouche is an Ardèche signature dish, delicious and well suited for cool days. Traditionally, this dish was cooked when a pig was slaughtered on the farm, but now it is more practical to buy the pork stomach at the wholesaler or butcher, such as Monsieur Chaniac at St.Etienne de Fontbellon. If you buy all your meat there, he'll throw in the stomach for you!

Serves 6 to 8

1kg onions
1kg Swiss chard or spinach
1kg sausage meat
800g pork belly
Pepper, salt
Four Spice (pepper, cloves, nutmeg and ginger)
1 pig's stomach

Cut the green of the Swiss chard leaves into thin strips and chop the onions finely. Cut the pork belly into small cubes and mix it all together with the sausage meat. Add the seasonings and mix well. Spoon the mixture into the pork stomach so that it is just over half full. Sew up the stomach with a strong thread and prick a couple of times so it does not burst while cooking. If you really want to play it safe, then also place it in a thin cotton sac. Carefully put the Pouytrole into a pan of boiling salted water (enough to cover it) and cook it for three hours without a lid. Keep adding more water so that it stays covered. Before serving, heat the Pouytrole in the oven so that it develops a lovely brownish colour

To serve, cut it into slices of about 1 inch and serve hot with a bit of vinegar and a mixed salad.

35. La Courgettine

This rice dish is an Ardèche version of Pilaf. You easily can make this into a vegetarian main course. It is easy to cook and surprisingly tasty.

Serves 8

5 to 6 medium courgettes
150g rice
300ml chicken stock or vegetable stock to make a vegetarian dish
3 eggs
190g Mimolette cheese; a soft cheese similar to Edam cheese
200ml Crème Fraiche or sour cream
1 tsp ground cumin
Salt and pepper

Put the rice into an ovenproof dish. Prepare the stock and pour it over the rice and set aside. Then, roughly peel the courgettes and grate them and the mimolette cheese. In a large bowl beat the eggs together with the crème fraiche and season according to taste with salt, pepper and cumin. Mix everything under the rice. Preheat the oven to 220° and cook for at least 30 minutes.

36. Pork Sausages

n the Ardèche, cooking revolved around the pig, appropriately named King of the Countryside. It allowed many generations to subsist and thus, the 'Tuade' or day of slaughter was a great feast. Everyone came to help and nothing was left over once the Cailletes, Black Pudding and the many different kind of sausages were prepared. Today, health and safety regulations make it almost impossible to slaughter a pig at home and the non commercial use of this craft is almost extinct. Mado now buys the guts and the pork shoulder already minced at her butcher's. The old recipes remain the same, however, and the sausages as delicious.

Ingredients for an extended family:

8.5kg pork shoulder
Guts - natural or artificial
Salt (16 gram per kg) and pepper
A good food processor

Untie the guts in warm water; then cut several pieces of about 1 to 2 metres and rinse them so that the warm water runs through. Make a knot at each end. Be careful that the guts stay moist and warm throughout the process. Spread out the minced meat, season with salt and pepper and mix well with your hands. Place a funnel on the mincing machine and pull an end of a gut over it. Press the meat through the machine into the gut down to the knotted end. When filled, close with a piece of string. To begin with, the sausages are very long. Fold them in two, squeeze and twist. Then go down about 15 cm on each side, squeeze, twist and make a loop. Repeat this further down until the end of the two halves. Repeat until you have used all the meat. Place the sausage loops on a towel before conserving them.

When this was done on the farm, the sausages were left to dry for several weeks in an airy attic to preserve them and make them tender. However, if in your loft ants, mice or birds could get to the sausages, it is advisable to keep them in your freezer.

Cook in the oven for half an hour at 200° or boiled in water for 20 minutes. Serve with good country bread and a glass of Merlot.

37. Pumpkin in Papillotte

The ideal time to make pumpkin in foil is when the weather is changing in the autumn. This is an original dish that looks very attractive. One small pumpkin is a very generous helping for one person and our ingredients are for one pumpkin only.

1 small pumpkin
1 medium size onion
2 slices of prosciutto or cured ham
2 slices of cooked ham
100g smoked bacon in cubes
250ml Creme Fraiche or sour cream
1 tsp ground cumin
Salt and pepper

Finely slice the onions and fry them in a bit of olive oil in a pan. Cut the cured ham and the cooked ham into thin strips. In a bowl, mix together the onions, the hams, the smoked bacon cubes and the sour cream. Add the cumin and stir well. Add pepper and a little salt.

Cut the top off the pumpkin as if it were a hat. Cut into the pumpkin with a curved knife and take out all the seeds with a spoon, but leave the flesh on the pumpkin. Stuff it with the ham and onion mixture. Place the 'hat' on the pumpkin and wrap it in aluminium foil.

Preheat the oven to 250° and leave to cook for at least 50 minutes. In order to test whether it is cooked through lift the 'hat' and plunge a knife into the flesh of the pumpkin. Once it is soft, take it out. It is important that the skin does not break.

Our suggestion: add a small handful of Porcini or Chanterelle mushrooms to the stuffing.

38. Crique

The Crique is one of the quintessential dishes of the Ardèche. There are hundreds of variations of this flat cake of grated raw potatoes, garlic and eggs. For a good Crique, it is important to make it crispy on the outside and soft on the inside. You'll see that this dish is easy and fast and can even be made in advance. It is an important contribution to any picnic. We have used Arlie potatoes because of their taste, their distinct white-pink colouring and because they are grown on the Plateau ardéchois.

One Crique serves as an excellent side dish for three to four people.

420g potatoes (or 3 big ones)
2 eggs
½ bunch fresh parsley
2 cloves of garlic
Salt & pepper

Peel the potatoes and grate them and immediately add salt to prevent browning. Mix the potatoes with the beaten eggs, the pepper, the squashed garlic cloves and the parsley. Heat vegetable oil in a small non-stick frying pan and shape the potato mix into small flat cakes. Brown the Crique well – at least 5 minutes - on one side then, turn over with the help of a lid and repeat on the other side.

Decorate with parsley and serve hot or warm with a crispy salad.

39. Guinea Fowl with Cabbage

The Guinea Fowl has a firm and tasty meat with a delicate flavour. This bird, whose origin is in Africa, is first mentioned in France during the Renaissance. Rabelais, in his book 'Pantagruel' speaks of the 'Guynette' or 'Poule de Guinée'. Its meat is finer, but also drier than that of chicken and certainly has less fat. The cabbage, on the other hand, is a common vegetable from Eastern and Southern Europe. The two flavours combine wonderfully and this dish has become an important part of the Ardèche cuisine.

1 guinea fowl
20g butter
1 green cabbage or Kale
300g bacon – smoked or unsmoked
1 big onion
1 glass of white wine
Salt and pepper

While you prepare the cabbage, place the guinea fowl in the oven with a bit of butter and let it brown. You could also do this in a pan, but it will take more time. While the bird is in the oven, cut the cabbage into fine strips and blanch them in boiling salted water for 5 to 6 minutes. Take out and drain well. Cut the bacon and the onion into small cubes and let them sweat together in a pan. Remove the bacon and place on a kitchen towel to let the fat come out. Add the cabbage to the pan with the onions and cook for another 10 minutes. Add the bacon pieces and salt and pepper. Cook over low heat for another 10 minutes. Once the guinea fowl has a golden-brown colour, place it in the pan with the cabbage. Cover with a lid and cook the guinea fowl and cabbage over low heat for 1 hour 20 minutes. It is important to occasionally take off the cover and baste the guinea fowl with white wine.

40. Smoothie with Saffron

S moothies are not typically from the Ardèche, but saffron grows well in these parts and Bruno Lebrun cultivates it on his land above Largentière. He and his wife Nathalie are continuously seeking new ways of utilising the stigmas of this small and amazing plant, the Crocus sativus, commonly known as the Saffron Crocus. The smoothie tastes great on a hot day and you can make it more liquid by replacing the yoghurt with soya milk or green tea.

Serves 6

4 big white peaches
6 ripe apricots
5 tbs ground almonds
3 tbs sugar
2 yoghurts, large
1 pinch of cinnamon
20 - 25 pistils of saffron
Sliced almonds to decorate

Soak the saffron threads for a while in a bit of water; place the fruit, the sugar, the cinnamon, the ground almonds and the yoghurts in a blender and mix well. At the end, add half the stigmas of saffron and mix again. Leave to rest in the fridge for at least 1 hour so that the saffron gives off its taste.

Serve the smoothie in glasses and decorate with the remainder of the saffron and the sliced almonds.

41. Gâteau Ardèchois

This cake with sweet chestnut puree or Crème de Marrons is soft inside and crispy on the outside. It evokes a sense of countryside and of good home cooking by the use of simple ingredients that are of the highest quality. It is quick and easy to make and, with a bit of rum added, will also be easy to consume.

500g crème de marrons (chestnut puree)
175g sugar
175g flour
175g butter
1tsp yeast
3 eggs
2tbs rum

Preheat the oven to 200 °. Mix the butter with flour, sugar, yeast, crème de marrons and the egg yolks in a mixer. Beat the egg whites until they are very stiff. Fold them carefully into the chestnut mixture and fill into a buttered and floured cake tin. Bake for 45 to 50 minutes.

Decorate with icing sugar and serve with either a dry white wine or with champagne.

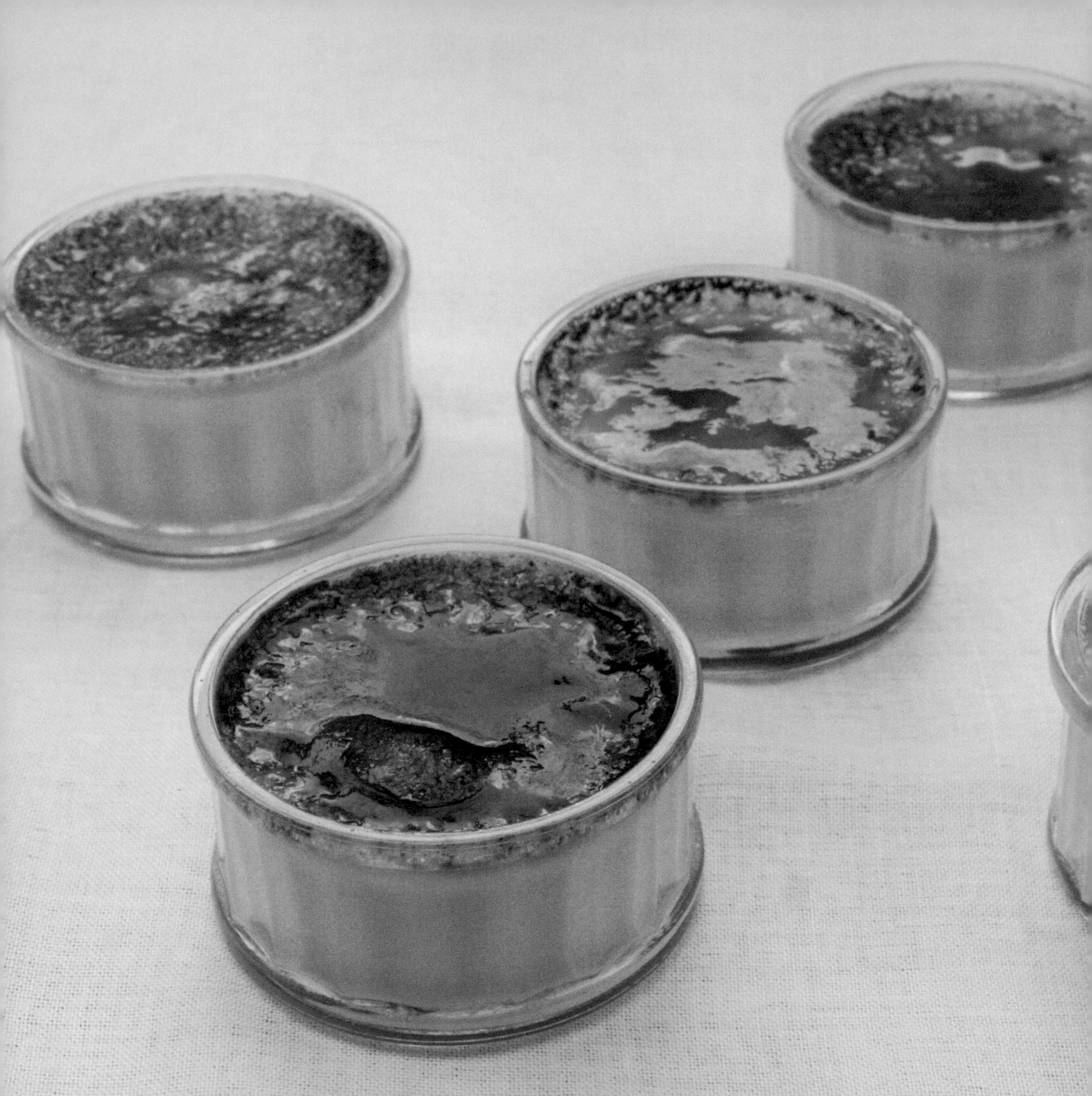

42. Crème Brulée with Saffron

The origins of the Crème Brulée are contested: the Spanish claim it since the 18th century as their 'Crema Catalana'. The British know for sure that 'Burnt Cream' was invented in Trinity College in Cambridge in the 17th century. Yet, in the 19th century the desert became French and fashionable in elegant houses from Paris to New York. The Ardèchois likely will say that they invented the version with saffron.

Serves 8 to 10

750ml double cream
250ml milk
200g caster sugar
10 egg yolks
12 saffron stigmas (6 for cooking and 6 to decorate)
Brown sugar

Bring the milk and the cream to boiling point. Take off the heat and leave to infuse with the 6 saffron pistils for 1 hour. Beat the egg yolks with the sugar until they become creamy white. Then add the saffron-milk. Pour into small ovenproof soufflé dishes, place 1 pistil at the centre of each dish and cook in the oven at 80° for 45 minutes. Take out of the oven and leave to cool. Then place it in the fridge for 1 to 2 hours. Sprinkle with brown sugar and caramelise with a gas flame.

43. Ice Cream with Crème de Marron

420g condensed Milk (unsweetened)
500g chestnut purée (sweet)

The night before, place the condensed milk in its tin in the refrigerator. The next day, whip it up until quite stiff and mix with the chestnut purée. Add a few broken 'marrons glacés' (glazed chestnuts) to the mixture. Put all of it into a savarin ring mold and place it in the freezer for at least 4 hours.

Serve with a sauce made of 100g of melted dark chocolate and 200ml double cream.

44. Puff Pastry

Once you have tried making your own puff pastry, you might also want to make a lighter - less buttery -version of this very fine and versatile pastry. For the 'half-butter' putt pastry, one literally takes half the butter for the same quantity of flour and instead of folding it 6 times, one turns it over 8 to 9 times, which produces the flaky effect. This is a messy process so it is advisable to keep a basin with soapy water on the side.

250g flour
250g butter
150ml water
1 pinch salt

Sift the of flour onto a table; make a hole, add salt, water and with your hands carefully work them into the flour so that the dough does not become ropy. Roll it into a ball and leave to rest for ¼ hour.

During this time, work the butter (with your hands during winter and in a fine linen cloth during summer). Place the dough onto the floured table, pressing it down by tapping it with your palm and at the same time forming a rectangle. Do the same with the butter; you might want to place it on cling film first and then onto the pastry. Lift the 4 corners of the pastry over the centre of the butter, close enough so that you can stick them together and enclose the butter completely; sprinkle with flour. Then, with a rolling pin, flatten this paste so that it makes a piece at least 3 times as long as it is wide. Fold over the opposite end to about 2/3rds of the length; fold the opposite end over it so that the dough is folded in three; leave for 15 minutes, flatten again into a rectangle and repeat this whole operation 6 times. Ten minutes after the last folding action, the dough is ready to be baked. It needs approximately 40 minutes at 180° in the oven with its filling.

Once you have tried your hand in making your own puff pastry, you might want to make a lighter – less buttery – version. For the 'half-butter' puff pastry, one literally takes half the butter for the same quantity of flour and instead of folding it 6 times, one turns it over 8 to 9 times, which produces the flaky effect. Both versions freeze really well.

45. Lemon Tart with Strawberries

Use the same traditional puff pastry recipe and once it is baked, fill it with lemon curd and strawberries. The lemon curd is an English speciality without which one cannot imagine many of the wonderful puddings of the English cuisine. If you make it yourself, it will taste more lemony and be less sweet. It will keep at least a month in the fridge.

For approximately 450 g of lemon curd:

2 large lemons – juice and grated rind
3 eggs
4oz butter
8oz sugar

Beat the eggs lightly and mix in the lemon rind and juice, butter and sugar. Place in the top of a double boiler or Bain Marie. Heat gently, stirring occasionally until the sugar has dissolved and the curd thickens. Leave to cool. Much of it will be used for the cake. Pour any surplus into small, clean and dry jars. Cover immediately and refrigerate.

For the garnish:
Take one 500 g punnet of strawberries and cut them into halves. Make a syrup with 250 ml or 1 cup of water and 100 g sugar. Let it boil for a couple of minutes, watching it all the time. It should not go brown. Add the juice of 1 lime and pour the boiling syrup over the strawberries.

Once the pastry is baked and cooled down, cover it with a layer of about 1 cm of lemon curd and then add the strawberries without too much of their juice.

46. Chocolate and Chestnut Cake

The chestnut is called Maroni once it is used in patisserie. However, in order to get to the good part of the chestnut, one has to peal off the hard outer skin with the help of a small, very sharp curved knife. The second and softer skin only comes off after the Maroni have been steamed and are still boiling hot. This will be painful for your fingers but well worth the effort. Then the small creases have to be cleaned before the fruit can be processed into wonderful sweet or salty dishes.

This rich cake has a subtle taste of chestnuts and a consistency like brownies.

500g chestnut cream (sweetened)
4 medium eggs
200g good dark chocolate
125g butter

Preheat the oven to 180°, gas mark 4. Melt the chocolate in the microwave or in a Bain Marie; add the butter in small pieces and let it melt into the chocolate; add the chestnut cream and with a wooden spoon gently draw it into the chocolate mixture; then add the eggs yolks one by one.

It is best to use a square cake mould. This will make it easier to cut the cake into small squares. Grease it with butter and powder it with flour. Beat the egg whites very stiff and fold them gently into the chestnut mixture. Pour into the mould and spread it out gently.

Bake it for a minimum of 30 minutes and test from time to time with the point of a knife The cake is ready when the knifepoint comes out clean.

Leave the cake to cool off, but take it out of the mould while still quite hot.

This cake can be eaten cold or warm and we suggest serving it with a lemon sorbet.

47. Apricot Cake

There are plenty of apricot trees in the Ardèche and this fruit announces the summer.

150g flour
700g apricots
40g butter
10g caster sugar
1 egg yolk
2tbs water

Heap the flour onto the table; make a hole in the middle and add the softened butter in small knobs. Work this with your hands; add the sugar, the egg yolk and a bit of water. Work the dough again and make a ball, which you leave to rest for 1 hour.

Butter and flour a cake mould and roll out the dough until it is about 3 mm thick; cover the mould completely.

Cut the apricots in halves, take out the stones and place the apricot pieces tightly onto the dough. Once the mould is full, sprinkle 2 tablespoons of sugar over the fruit.

Preheat the oven to 180° and bake the tart for about ¼ hour. After this, take it out of its mould and leave to cool on a baking tray.

48. Flambéed Figs

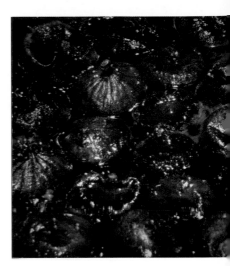

Nada brought this recipe to perfection on the beaches of the Côte d'Azur in the glamorous 70s. Now, as a gardener in the Ardèche, he found out that the figs in our garden are of the right sort. He re-invented the recipe and each time we are surprised by his skills as a chef. The best figs for this desert are the red or 'Muscat' ones. If they are perfectly ripe, you don't need to cut them in halves. The result will be a beautiful dish.

Serves 6

30 medium Muscat figs
100g butter
2 oranges, juiced
3tbs brown sugar
1tbs cinnamon
1tbs orange peel, grated
Cognac for flaming

Cook the figs in the butter in a wide frying pan for ¼ hour covered with a lid. Sprinkle them with sugar and cook for another ¼ hour or until the sugar starts to caramelise. Then, add the orange juice and sprinkle with cinnamon. Lower the heat, cover with the lid and leave to simmer in their juice for another ¼ hour. This preparation can be done in advance.

Before serving the figs, heat them well while basting continuously with their juice.

Sprinkle with the grated orange rind and then with the cognac and ignite it with a long match.

Serve hot with a glass of chilled Montbazillac or with pink champagne.

49. Orange and Apple Pie

n the winter the House of Sabaton in Aubenas (Ardèche) sells masses of peeled oranges, because they only need the peels for making their famous candied peel of oranges. This abundance helped us to create the recipe.

Serves 8

For the shortcrust pastry:

250g flour, sifted
125g butter, softened
1 pinch salt and a bit of water

For the filling:

4 apples, cut into thin slices and cooked 4 minutes in the microwave
3 oranges, peeled and without skin
2tbs ground almonds
2tbs double cream
3tbs icing sugar
1 egg

Mix the sifted flour and the butter relatively quickly between the tips of your fingers. Once the mixture is crumbly like couscous, add a bit of water in order to make a big dough ball. This needs to rest for about 1 hour. In the meantime, prepare the filling: mince the oranges with a mixer, and then add all the ingredients, except the apples, with the egg last. Mix again, but this time with a whisk. Spread the shortcrust pastry in a buttered tin and cover it with the cooked apples. Then pour in the orange mixture. Bake for about 30 minutes in a preheated oven at 180°, but keep on checking towards the end.

50. Quince Paste

Quinces have plenty of natural pectin, which makes them ideal for the preparation of jellies and fruit paste. This confectionary is prepared in autumn but can be enjoyed all year round. Like the Spanish membrillo, we prefer it as an accompaniment with hard cheeses, but traditionally it was eaten wrapped in granulated sugar as a sweet.

Preparation 2 hours. Cooking time 1h 50 minutes.

0.8 kg of jam sugar per kilogram of pulp
1 to 3 kg of pulp of quince and apples (80/20%)
Juice of 1 lemon
Muslin or some very fine cotton fabric and some fine string

To make the pulp: Rub the quinces with a cloth; cut them in pieces and take out the core. Keep the pips and, if possible, put them in a little bag. Together with the apple pieces and the sachet of pips, place the fruit in a large pan, cover with water and bring to a boil. Cook for 30 to 40 minutes until the quince pieces are quite soft. Then pour it through a fine sieve and take out the sachet of pips. Keep the juice if you want to make quince jelly. Press the fruit pieces through a blender or a sieve. You will get a brownish purée.

To make the quince paste: Weigh the purée and prepare 0.8 kg of sugar per kilogram of purée. Pour it all into a tall pan and cook over moderate heat for about 1 hour – continuously stirring with a wooden spoon. The paste must not stick to the bottom of the pan. Gradually, it will turn a beautiful amber colour and, at the end, will become very thick with exploding bubbles. Be careful not to burn yourself. Once the paste comes off the sides of the pan, take it off the heat. Prepare a several moulds and lay them out with baking paper and pour in the paste about 3 to 4 cm high. It gets harder once it cools. The paste should rest at least for 24 hours up to a couple of days. You can keep it for a long time in a cool and dry place.

51. Apple Tart with Thyme

For the purée:

8 cooking apples
1 packet of vanilla sugar
1 cup of raisins or sultanas

For the pastry:

200g flour
100g butter
Pinch of salt
2tsp caster sugar

For the topping:

2 big cooking apples cut into fine wedges
2 tbsp fresh thyme

Peel and core the apples and cook them, with the vanilla sugar and the raisins, with a little water over low heat until they form a thick purée.

Make the pastry in a mixer and add 3 to 4 tablespoons of water until the dough can be rolled into a ball. Knead it again.

Spread the pastry in a buttered and floured cake tin and fill with the purée. Place the apple wedges above the purée and powder with the thyme.

Bake in the oven at 200° for 40 minutes.

52. Acacia Fritters

Watch over the flowering of the Acacia or Locust Trees and make sure you are around to make this ephemeral dish. It is only during one or two weeks in Spring, until the flowers fade on the trees, that you will be able to make these refined fritters. There are so many Acacia trees in the Ardèche that on walk along a steep valley you can just pick the flowers with a big secateur.

Serves 4 or about 20 fritters

About 20 clusters of flowers
250g flour, sifted
5 eggs
250ml milk
125g butter, slightly salted
1 small glass (50 cl) of calvados or rum
3tbs icing sugar
1tsp vanilla extract
1 pinch of salt

Make sure that your acacia flowers are really dry. With an electric mixer, beat the softened butter together with the icing sugar, the vanilla extract and the salt. Add the flour bit by bit then add the eggs one by one while you continue mixing. Once the mixture is smooth, slowly add the milk and then the liqueur. Mix well. Heat the oil in a deep fryer. Once it seems hot enough, plunge the flowers one at a time into the dough, pull them out with their stalk and lower each one into the oil. Fry them in small batches in order not to lower the temperature of the oil too much. Once they are golden brown on both sides, retrieve them with a skimmer.

Place them on kitchen roll to absorb the fat. Choose a wide dish, sprinkle the acacia fritters with more icing sugar and serve warm.

Should you not have enough time to make the fritters when the flowers are in bloom, they freeze really well. You should place them frozen into the dough.

Goats Cheeses

The Ardèche is famous for its charcuterie, honey, marrons glacés (candied chestnuts), and the Caillette, but the one speciality not to be missed is local goat's cheese. Like the tastes of the cuisine of the Ardèche, the cheeses are very authentic and are an expression of the rurality of this region.

The plateau of the Ardèche has always played host to herds of goats. A relatively small number of 'producteurs' are rearing goats on their own farms and make the small creamy cheeses In the now very rare traditional knowledge of their forefathers. During a period of 20 hours they let the raw, full-cream goats' milk curdle at 20° with a tiny amount of rennet. After that they delicately place the curdled milk into 'faisselles', plastic molds with holes from which the cheeses get their shapes. During the draining period each cheese is turned at least once. The salting is done on both sides with table salt. At a later stage, the cheeses are taken out of their moulds and then are left to dry and ripen. 14 days after renneting, and if the producer is supervised, the cheeses can take the 'Appelation' Picodon and can be sold immediately or left to ripen through different stages until they become the wrinkled, strong and blackened little cheeses that will give your taste buds quite a shock the first time.

The region offers numerous superb goats' cheeses of which the Picodon has just been mentioned. Its taste is sweet and sharp, straightforward and subtle; it brings a taste of hazelnuts to the fore. Whilst maturing, a white natural crust with hues of blue covers the cheese. Then there are the Tommes and Tommettes, which are sweet and creamy and blend perfectly into any meal. As the Tommettte de Brobie – this is actually made from sheep's milk – matures, it is slowly covered by a floury grey crust that enhances all its aromas. And then there is the Chèvreton – a young cousin of the Picodon, with a shorter maturing time. It is a more unctuous type of cheese and is both sweeter-tasting and smaller and is perfect in cooking. And last but not least comes the very special Sarment d'amour. This is a cute goats' cheese on a branch or twig. The 'sarments de vigne' are the twigs from grapevines. The taste of the cheese is tangy and not overpoweringly goaty and it has that sort of thick, dry-creamy texture of a fabulous New York cheesecake. Because of the tiny bite-size and the handy little twigs, Sarments d'Amour are the only cheeses regularly served as aperitifs.

For over 30 years, Marie Josée and Claude Smets have been making excellent cheeses on their beautiful farm in Prunet. Here the sheep and goats enjoy one of the loveliest views over the valley. The speciality of Marie Josée and Claude are the Sarments d'Amour which they sell to famous cheese shops in Paris, such as Crémerie Barthélemy, and even export them to the UK and Japan. However, the best plan is to catch them at the market of Largentière, on Tuesday mornings where you can buy directly their prize-winning cheeses.

53. Green Tea with Saffron

This famous tea has a long list of virtues: it is supposed to be an aphrodisiac and good against hangovers; supposedly it helps with dieting; soothes period pains; and helps to get your energy back. In short, the effects of the tea have been compared to those of antidepressants. According to the saffron grower Bruno Lebrun, saffron's real qualities are that it is a natural dye and gives a wonderful colour to your food with an aroma that is considered seductive. Also, it harmonises and emphasizes the different flavours of your cuisine. These qualities alone are enticing. However, if you are not used to the taste, the tea can be a little bitter. Thus, it tastes great when served with very sweet biscuits.

1tbs honey
45 stigmas of Saffron
1 litre water
1tbs green tea leaves

Dilute one tablespoon of honey with one tablespoon of hot water and let the saffron stigmas infuse in the mixture. Warm your teapot with a bit of hot water, which you then throw out. Put the tea leaves into a tea infuser. First put the watery saffron pistils into the teapot; then non-boiling hot water and the tea infuser, which you take out after 5 minutes. Leave the saffron pistils a couple of minutes longer. Keep the tea leaves; you can use them a second time once your teapot is emptied.

54. Green Tea Jelly with Saffron

Bruno and Nathalie have converted the land around their house into a saffron field. The whole family and all those passing by chance are invited to help them with their new adventure – harvesting the delicate flowers, picking off the pistils with a squeezer, drying them in a special oven, stirring jams with saffron and testing exotic recipes. In order to set the jelly, we use the gelling agent agar-agar, which comes from the Malay name for a red algae called Gagartina.

3 litres water
10 small apples
2kg sugar
30 saffron pistils
3tbs green tea
1 packet Agar-agar

Prepare the saffron by soaking the pistils in a little bit of water. Cut the apples in quarters and cook them in water. Filter this compote. Mix the tea leaves into the filtered water and pour in the sugar. Mix and cook for ¼ hour. Take out the tea leaves and add the soaked agar-agar. Towards the end, pour the saffron into the jelly. Once the cooking is finished, pour the mix as hot as possible into jars or glasses, that have been washed and then sterilised in lots of boiling water for at least a couple of minutes. Let them drip dry upside down. Fill to the near the top with the jelly. Close the lids well and turn upside-down until completely cooled down. This eliminates oxygen and the potential of creating mould and is a good conservation process.

55. Orange Marmalade with Saffron

Even in France, there are countless recipes for orange marmalade. Ours is easy to make and has a wonderful homemade taste to it. It is best to use untreated Seville Oranges, which are bittersweet.

3kg oranges (peeled and skinned)
2kg sugar
1tbs agar-agar powder
40 saffron pistils

Peel and skin the oranges and cut them into thin slices. Leave to macerate with the sugar for a couple of hours. Prepare the pistils by soaking them in a little water. Spread the Agar-Agar in water and add to the oranges. Then, gently cook the oranges for one hour. Add the soaked saffron pistils ¼ hour before the end. As soon as the jam is finished, pour it into your sterilised jars or jam pots. Conserve the marmalade in the same procedure noted in recipe number 50.

This is the professional advice given by my friend Michael Jack: In order to arrive at a long shelf-life, jam makers should check the soluble solids content, which should ideally be 69 degrees brix. Then the available water is reduced so that bacteria and spores cannot grow; if less they may be able to. If the soluble solids (mostly sugar) are too high crystallisation may occur later. A brix refractometer is not very expensive, maybe €50 on Amazon etc. Experienced jam makers can get the parameters right without one, but maybe not all home confectioners will and quality, storage time and safety may then suffer.

56. Quince Jelly

Quinces are harvested from the end of September to mid November. When the fluff comes off easily with a towel and when their scent is strong, they are ripe. Their flavour goes well with those of apples, pears, cinnamon and poultry. One only consumes them cooked and they make wonderful jelly, jam, fruit paste and compote which go well with meat. They easily can be kept for several weeks at room temperature.

Preparation: 2 hours

20 ripe quinces for 6L of liquid
5kg jam sugar (0.8 kg per litre)
3 lemons (juice of ½ lemon per litre)
6 bags at 4grams of agar-agar (1 sachet per litre)

Brush and wash the quinces. Peel and take out the inner cores and keep the seeds. Put the skins, seeds and cores into a large pot, cover with water and cook slowly for ¾ to 1 hour. This depends on the hardness of the fruit. One can cook the fruit together with the skins and cores in order to later make quince paste. It is recommended to let it rest for one night and reheat it the next day.

To make the jelly, take out skins and cores (and fruit) from the liquid. Then strain it through a scalded jelly bag and leave to drip for at least 1 hour. Do not squeeze the bag, as this will cloud the jelly. Measure the quantity of the strained juice and add sugar, lemon and, at the very end, the agar-agar. In order to create a finer aroma, make the jelly in small quantities. Bring the juice and sugar to boiling point and boil rapidly for about 10 minutes or until setting point is reached. The jelly is ready if a drop jellifies on a small plate. Take the pan off the heat and remove any scum. Pour the mix into sterilised and still warm jars while it is hot and directly close the lids and leave to rest top down until the jelly has completely cooled off.

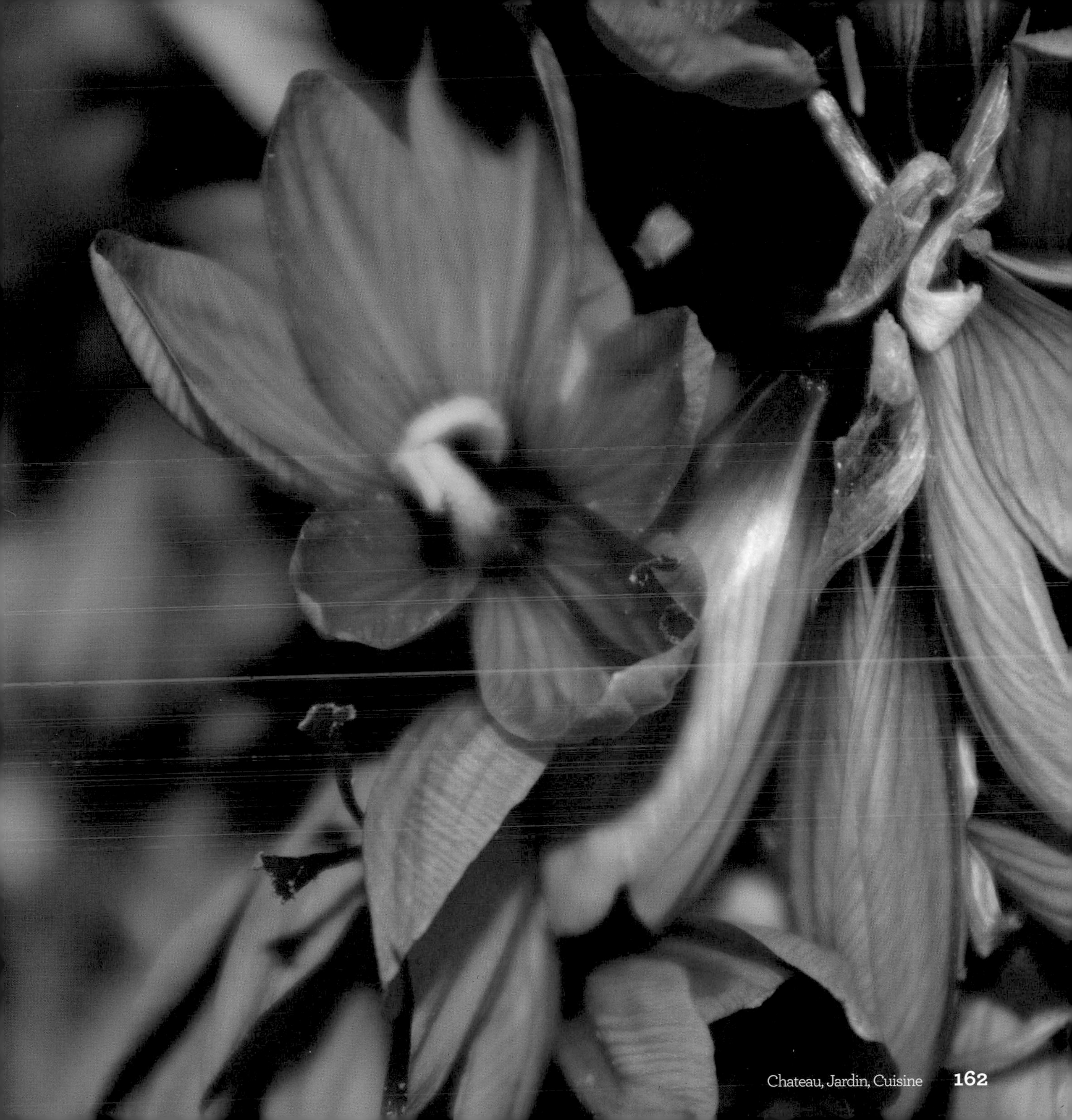

57. Pear Jam with Vanilla and Saffron

This jam is ideally made with the famous pears Abate Fétel. The abbot Fétel from Chessy-les–Mines in France discovered the seedling more or less by accident in 1866. The flesh of the pear is juicy and slightly musky. They are harvested between end of September and October and reach their natural ripeness by mid October. The taste of this jam is very delicate and it would qualify for the most elegant tea, but it might also just be perfect for the first 'tartine' in the morning, when one is still a bit delicate.

1.6kg pears (skinned and without core)
1kg sugar
1 vanilla pod
1tbs agar-agar
25 saffron pistils

Peel the pears, take out the cores and cut them in slices. Place them in a large bowl with the sugar and the vanilla pod, which has been cut lengthwise. Prepare the saffron pistils by soaking them in a little water. Sprinkle the Agar-Agar in water and bring to boil together with the pears, the sugar and the vanilla pod. Leave the jam to cook gently for about 30 minutes and 15 minutes before the end, pour in the saffron. As soon as this process is finished, pour the jam into jars. You will have sterilised them before for a couple of minutes in lots of boiling water and left to dry head down making sure, however, that they are completely dry. Once you have filled them with the still hot jam, close the lids immediately and turn upside down and leave to cool off completely. This will make a stable produce without further sterilisation.

58. Apricot Jam with Saffron

This recipe won a prize in a competition organised by the priest of the Catholic church of Gourdon in the Ardèche. Since a few years, this event has become a tradition and takes place on the 15th of August after mass. Every competitor brings a homemade jam and the selection of the winner takes place in a spirit of basic democracy, sharing and good taste. In the confusion it was impossible to be sure who had made this delicious jam, but we secured a copy of the recipe anyway.

3kg apricots
1.2kg sugar
1tsp bitter almond essence
1tsp agar-agar
60 pistils of saffron

Take the stones out of the apricots and leave the fruits to macerate with the sugar and the almond essence for two to three hours. Soak the saffron pistils in a small glass of water. Cook all together for about 30 minutes and add the agar-agar, which you have soaked in water, 15 minutes before the end.

Once the cooking is finished, pour the jam into jam jars or glasses. For good conservation, without resorting to the more labour intensive sterilisation, follow the same method as above.

59. Lemon Jelly

Very few people have the courage and willpower to make lemon jelly and it took Bruno Lebrun several years and dozens of trials to come up with a recipe that is reliable. Even in shops the jelly is not found very often and then it might taste artificial and can be too set. Bruno sells his in tiny pots at the organic market in Ruoms in the Ardèche near the Caverne du Pont d'Arc (http://en.cavernedupontdarc.fr). Both are worth the trip.

3L water
8 large lemons
2kg sugar
40 pistils of saffron
40g agar-Agar
4 lemon zests

Peel the lemons and keep the zest of four of them. Leave to macerate all eight lemons, the zest and the sugar in three litres of water for 24 hours. It is important to use a recipient of stainless steel in order to avoid any oxidation. The following day, place the pistils in a small amount of water and leave for a minimum of 20 minutes. In a large jam maker or copper casserole slowly heat up the lemon-sugar mix. Rehydrate the Agar-Agar in a little bit of water and then add to the lemons. Slowly bring the mixture to boiling point. Once there, leave it to bubble for 20 minutes at high temperature and stir with a wooden spoon so that the jelly does not stick to the walls or burn. Take off the froth that sets at the rims of the casserole and - after the 20 minutes are finished - add the saffron solution with the pistils and cook for another 10 minutes.

Immediately, fill the jelly into jars - as described in the recipes above - and place them upside down until cool. Then, all there is left to do is to enjoy this unique jelly at breakfast with butter on toast or at teatime as a topping on cakes.

60. Ice cream with Basil

Serves 6

5 egg yolks
150g & 50g sugar
400ml milk
250ml cream
1 bunch of basil
700g red berries or fruit
Juice of 2 oranges
½ tsp Pastis liqueur

Bring the milk to the boil and once away from the heat, add 20 basil leaves and leave them to infuse for 10 minutes. During this time, beat the egg yolks with 150 grams of sugar until the cream gets a whitish colour. Pour in the milk without the basil leaves and mix well. Bring the mixture to the boil over low to moderate heat and let simmer while stirring constantly until it thickens and coats the back of a spoon. Take off the heat and add the cream. Once the mixture has cooled down, mix in the Pastis and 20 finely cut basil leaves, new ones of course. Place in an icecream maker or in the freezer for at least 4 hours.

For the fruit salad, prepare the fruit by washing them slightly and place them in a dish with the 50 grams of sugar and the orange juice. Add 10 finely cut basil leaves, mix well and keep in a cool place. This wonderful ice cream could also be served with a peach fruit salad.

First published by Unicorn
an imprint of Unicorn Publishing Group LLP, 2019
5 Newburgh Street
London W1F 7RG
www.unicornpublishing.org

All rights reserved. No part of the contents of this book may be
reproduced, stored in or introduced into a retrieval system, or
transmitted, in any form or by any means (electronic, mechanical,
photocopying, recording or otherwise), without the prior written
permission of the copyright holder and the above publisher of this book.

Every effort has been made to trace copyright holders and to obtain
their permission for the use of copyright material. The publisher
apologises for any errors or omissions in the above list and would be
grateful if notified of any corrections that should be incorporated in
future reprints or editions of this book.

Text © Regina von Planta, 2019
Photographs © Regina von Planta, 2019

10 9 8 7 6 5 4 3 2 1

ISBN 978-1-912690-29-9

Design by Jonathan Richards
Cover design by Unicorn Publishing Group
Printed in India by Imprint Press